Joseph A. Payne, O.P.

Befriending

A Self-Guided Retreat
for Busy People

PAULIST PRESS
New York/Mahwah, N.J.

INTERIOR ILLUSTRATIONS: KATHLEEN FISKE

Library of Congress Cataloging-in-Publication Data

Payne, Joseph A., 1934–
    Befriending: a self-guided retreat for busy people/Joseph A. Payne.
        p.   cm.
    Includes bibliographical references.
    ISBN 0-8091-3354-7 (paper)
    1. Friendship—Religious   aspects—Christianity—Meditations.   2. Spiritual life—Catholic   Church.   3. Catholic   Church—Membership.   4. Retreats.
    I. Title.
    BV4647.F7P39   1992
    241′.676—dc20   92-28398
                                                                                                      CIP

Published by Paulist Press
997 Macarthur Boulevard
Mahwah, NJ 07430

Printed and bound in the
United States of America

Contents

DEDICATION

In loving memory of
my mother and father,
best friends of each other,
who taught me much of what
they knew about loving

Acknowledgments

Many people played a significant part in my life during the writing of this book. I would like to thank the following in a special way:

My provincial, Father Thomas J. Ertle, OP, for providing the sabbatical during which I did much of the writing.

The Dominican community and my former peers on the staff of St. Stephen Priory Spiritual Life Center in Dover, Massachusetts, for their love, encouragement and apostolic enthusiasm.

Father Gene Konkel, SS, of the Vatican II Institute in Menlo Park, California, who welcomed me into the renewal program during which my ideas became focused.

The Dominican nuns of the Monastery of Mary the Queen in Elmira, New York, who provided for me a marvelous space in which to write, encouraged me by their example, strengthened me by their prayer, and even snickered during many of my early morning homilies.

Paul Wilkes, the author, who shared his considerable gifts and advised and encouraged me over the course of my writing; Paula Carroll, who taught me about the details of editing a manuscript; and Mrs. Kathy Fiske, who agreed to enhance this text with her lovely drawings.

Father Paul Philibert, OP, my friend and classmate, and Archbishop Thomas C. Kelly, OP, of Louisville, for their brotherly enthusiasm for this project; and Father Paul Lucey, SJ, of Boston and Father Martin, OSB, prior of Mount Savior Monastery of Elmira, New York, who were my spiritual directors during the writing.

The close friends who read the early drafts of my chapters, encouraged me, and gave me very honest feedback and countless helpful suggestions.

My brother Bob, his wife Joan, and their family, who affirmed what I was doing and continued to give me the sturdy example of their love for each other.

The Dominican community, staff and people of St. Louis Bertrand Parish in Louisville, Kentucky, for their welcome of me during the latter part of my writing.

And finally, and most gratefully, Father Dick Sparks, CSP, my editor at Paulist Press, for his expertise and unfailing good humor from start to finish.

Introduction

Brenda Ueland, in her salty little book *If You Want To Write,* has a chapter entitled "Why a Renaissance Nobleman Wrote Sonnets" in which she says:

> A Renaissance nobleman wrote a love sonnet for a number of reasons. A slight and very incidental reason may have been that he wanted to show people he could do it. But the main reason was to tell a certain lady that he loved her. . . .[1]

She adds, "One of the intrinsic rewards for writing the sonnet was that then the nobleman . . . knew more about what love was. . . ."

For some years now, though quite unlike a "Renaissance nobleman," I have wanted to write. I have wanted to show people I could do it and to show *myself* that I could do it. Mostly I have wanted to share something of what I have learned about love, and I knew that in the process of writing, I would learn more about loving.

During my three decades of ministry in hospitals, religious formation, and vocations, in retreats in various places, recently for seven years at St. Stephen Priory Spiritual Life Center in Dover, Massachusetts, and now as pastor of St. Louis Bertrand Parish in Louisville, Kentucky, it has become increasingly clear to me that people *wonder if they are lovable* and they *want to know how to love.*

So I write. For years the themes I share have been resounding in me. As they have resounded, the theme of love has become more prominent. Now I need to listen again to this song of love. I need to listen to its cadences and elaborate its chords. I need to compose some variations on this theme of love. My hope is that in showing that I can do it, I may keep learning how to love, "show" how beautiful love is, and help others to love in an enhanced fashion.

Over the past few years something new started to show up in my preaching—the idea of *being befriended* and of *befriending*. Often when I thought back over a homily I had given, I would notice that without having planned to do so, I had spoken again about "befriending." So now, in terms of the great commandment, the commandment to love, I want to share with you at some length insights into this marvelous reality: God befriends us by sending us Jesus; Jesus calls each of us his friend, and teaches us both how to be friends with God and how to be friends with each other. Jesus reminds us tellingly of God's love for us, and wants to firmly convince us of our own lovableness. Jesus wants us to learn how to love God, ourselves, and our neighbors, his other friends. But for this befriending to occur in a creative, ongoing fashion, we need to foster a contemplative, thoughtful attitude; we need to learn how to retreat!

Befriending and the Practice of Retreating

Retreating is a Christian practice as old as the gospels. Jesus regularly left the crowds and went—by himself—to the lakeside or to the mountain. He also gathered his disciples for times of prayer and reflection. Since the time of Jesus, some of his followers have left for the desert and some have left for the monastery. Others, lay and religious, have gone to places of retreat for a shorter time—to a lake, mountain or seashore, or to a retreat house. More frequently, they have simply gone to their own rooms and shut their doors.

We benefit by retiring from the day-to-day routine of life in order to be refreshed, to gain perspective, to put things in order. For the busier among us the chance to get away for a while, even a short while, fills a rather desperate need. Those who staff retreat houses continually welcome folks who seem to be at the point of exhaustion. Often, about halfway through their retreat, they become rested enough to really begin. Almost unanimously at the end of their retreat people say that they wish the time had been longer; they don't feel ready to return to their daily schedules.

This book is written with the conviction that Christian life is meant to have a restful dimension to it, that all believers need both an appropriate place and sufficient time to ponder the meaning of their lives. Place and time—under "retreat" Webster addresses both. *Place:* "a safe, quiet, or secluded place." *Time:* "a period of retirement or seclusion, esp. one devoted to religious contemplation away from the pressures of ordinary life. . . ."[2] Webster lists also a military term—"beat a retreat": "to signal for retreat *by beating a drum*" (italics mine). My hope is that in what follows, you who live in situations filled with pressure will find help in your efforts to "beat a retreat," to beat your own retreat drum. My hope is that you will find retreat times of whatever duration, retreat places of whatever kind, where you will, in an ongoing way, "ponder the meaning of it all," and learn more about love and befriending.

But retreating well demands practice and an embrace of those elements important for retreats. Let me suggest some of them, both for individuals and for married couples and friends who wish to retreat together.

Sacred Time

All time is, of course, holy. God gifts us with this "little time" before we meet Jesus again at the end of our time, the beginning of our time. To be reflective, "thought-full," during our sacred time is not always easy, however. We need to claim our time; unclaimed, it tends to evaporate, to dissipate. We claim our time by managing our calendar, which represents whatever is of priority for us: appointments, tasks, meetings with friends. We need to monitor our pattern of choices, to look back at recent months to see whether or not we had sufficient time for prayer, rest, and retreat. It's helpful, also, to look ahead. Some people have a simple appointment book for planning their retreating time and their time for nourishment and for fun. They look ahead and set aside in their calendars a daily time for prayer, an occasional relaxed weekend, an afternoon of quiet, a monthly "desert day" or weekly holy hour.

You might choose to celebrate the seasons of the year: some time each spring, summer, fall, and winter to savor the gift of each season. You might celebrate liturgical seasons, with some special time each Advent, Christmas, Lent, Easter, and Pentecost to ponder the meaning these holy times are meant to have. You might reflect on your personal seasons: birthdays, anniversaries of marriage, of religious profession, of the death of a spouse, family member, or close friend. In these and many other ways you can so manage your calendar that you will experience more fully the sacredness of your time.

Sacred Space

Our surroundings can have a powerful impact on us. People who live near water or near the desert or the mountains have it made! Some of the rest of us may at least be able to get to a lovely spot regularly. Local or state parks are possibilities. Perhaps you have a yard to which you can go, or a window through which you can enjoy a sunrise or sunset or bright moon. Maybe there's a room in your place that will yield a prayer corner to which you can retreat. Perhaps you have a bedroom with a chair that can become your sacred space, a place for prayer and quiet. Or you can simply take an ordinary chair and turn it at a different angle, dedicating it to your thoughtful purpose for a few minutes. You can enhance your sacred space by having there a small crucifix, an icon or holy card, a plant, a bible, a candle.

Sacred Reading

God's self-revelation to us in sacred scripture is at the heart of Christian spirituality. Have your bible near, then, during times of retreat. Spiritual writers are often very helpful too, of course; many of us have been touched deeply by both contemporary and classical authors. It is important to remember, though, that spiritual authors depend, as we do, on God's revealing activity, and that by sharing their insights, they mean to help us to find God directly, especially in the word.

A Journal

As you spend reflective retreat time you find that you come to a deeper awareness of God's presence and of the fuller meaning of your life in Jesus. Personal themes begin to sound within you. A spiritual journal provides the opportunity for you to dwell upon these themes by writing about them. The writing is simply an aid to your interior growth.

There are highly developed approaches to journaling, and these can be very helpful (cf. Ira Progoff [3]). There are also very simple ways of keeping a journal. You might buy a spiral notebook of a size that doesn't overwhelm you; this can help make journaling feel accessible. If you are drawn to something a bit more formal, you might invest in one of the manuscript books, those bound personal journals available in many bookstores.

On a given day you might merely write out in your journal the scripture verses you have prayed over. Or you might, after your time of prayer, compose a personal prayer or write about how God has spoken to you and where God is calling you. You might occasionally write a letter to God, as one of my friends does, or a letter to a person, alive or deceased, with whom you need to be more fully reconciled. You might muse over a poem or a lovely thought, or list some of your joys or heartaches.

Spiritual Guidance/Spiritual Friendship

To foster clarity in your retreating, it can be very helpful to speak with someone about what you experience. The Christian community has a marvelous tradition of spiritual guidance in which two believers meet to reflect upon God's presence in one of their lives (sometimes called "spiritual direction"). More recently the possibility of "spiritual friendship," in which the guidance is mutual, has been suggested.[4] In either case, the focus is upon God's presence and God's activity in a person's life, and her or his response in prayer and action.

Wives and husbands, friends, community members and parishioners can be spiritual friends to each other. People who share a particular spiritual heritage (e.g. that of Francis, Julie Billiart, Dominic, Benedict, Catherine McCauley) can be of special help to each other in appropriating their common tradition.

Persons who have had the opportunity for spiritual guidance or who have experienced the spiritual friendship of which I speak will be familiar with some of the material I present. Hopefully they too will find here some fresh insights. People who have not experienced spiritual guidance or spiritual friendship may find here some of what they might otherwise have had.

Design of This Book

In the chapters that follow we will touch upon some of the many facets of love in our lives. Because God took the initiative in loving, we'll reflect first on *God's love for us,* befriending us, sending Jesus to convince us that we are loved, and asking our response. We'll reflect upon the call to *love God* by befriending God's word and also by recognizing and befriending God's presence in both contemplative and active times.

After the consideration of God's love for us and our love of God, we'll dwell upon the command to *love ourselves.* We'll think about our call to befriend our life stories as well as our own selves, and to befriend God's call to us.

Next, we'll reflect on our call to *love our neighbor,* those close to us, those who are strange to us and who feel like enemies to us, and those near and far to whom we are continually sent, missioned.

Finally, we'll ponder our call to *befriend the earth* and its many creatures.

In each chapter, after sharing my own reflections on some aspect of befriending, of living the great commandment, I will suggest scripture passages for your prayer to help you to dwell upon additional aspects of the theme presented. It will be helpful for you to read each passage in its broader context in your own bible.

I will also offer citations from non-scriptural sources, both from our Christian heritage and from contemporary authors. I do this with the belief that all that is true has its source in God, and that the Holy Spirit, the Spirit of love, can use it to teach us to love.

Finally, at the end of each chapter I will suggest some ways of praying over the themes presented, some "moments of retreat." These suggestions are meant only to promote your own unique prayerful response to the themes presented and to foster your ongoing embrace of the command to love, of the call to be befriended and to befriend. As to how you employ this book, I encourage you to be creative. Trust the promptings of the Spirit, pausing over those thoughts that engage you, and returning to those themes which seem personally most fruitful. The task for each of us throughout our lives is, of course, not only to honor our holy thoughts and creative insights, but also to embrace the life of love which they suggest. My hope and prayer is that you will use this text in a way which will enhance that ongoing embrace in your life.

NOTES

1. Brenda Ueland, *If You Want To Write,* Second Edition (Saint Paul: Graywolf Press, 1987), 17.
2. *Webster's New World Dictionary of the American Language,* Second College Edition (New York: Simon and Schuster, 1980), 1215.
3. Ira Progoff, *At a Journal Workshop* (New York: Dialogue House Library, 1975).
4. Tilden Edwards, *Spiritual Friend* (New York: Paulist Press, 1980), 106.

CHAPTER I

Letting Jesus Befriend You

"I have called you friends"
JOHN 15:15

Jesus came to convince us that God loves us. Imagine for a moment that at a point in time word got back to God that many of us, even though we possessed marvelous personal gifts and were surrounded by a world of tremendous beauty, were still unsure about God's love for us. So God designed a plan to make God's love much more obvious to us, much more convincing. The plan involved sending the only Son to live within an ordinary family setting for many years, and then to walk openly among us, God's people, for three short years. Jesus came, then, and lived among us. Jesus told us how much God loves us. Jesus gave sight to our blind, gait to our lame, speech to our mute, peace to our troubled. Jesus forgave our sins, gave us food and drink, embraced our children, cried and laughed with us, and told us about the reign of God.

All along the way, Jesus touched a wide variety of us: those who fish, practice law, are public officials, parents, widows, tax collectors, and prostitutes. He welcomed us; he was very approachable. If we found it hard to go to him, he reached out to us. He sought us out when our friends told him of our special needs. Jesus *befriended* us and wanted us to let him befriend us. He loved us as a friend would love us, in ways that were obvious: there were wedding feasts, banquets, picnics on a hillside, rides in boats, tears when people died, and safety for those under attack. His love was an empathic love, a tangible, visible love. We did not need to analyze his feelings for us. We knew that he loved us, because he loved us in unmistakable ways.

Jesus also taught us. Remember some of the things he wanted us to learn about love:

> Just then a lawyer stood up to test Jesus. "Teacher," he said, "what must I do to inherit eternal life?" He said to him, "What is written in the law? What do you read there? He answered, "You shall love the Lord your God with all your heart, and with all your soul, and with all your strength, and with all your mind; and your neighbor as yourself." And he said to him, "You have given the right answer; do this, and you will live."
>
> *Luke 10:25–28*

In the gospels of Matthew (Matthew 22:34–40) and Mark (Mark 12:28–34), Jesus is asked which is the greatest of all the commandments, and in response he cites two texts from the Old Testament:

> Hear, O Israel: The Lord is our God, the Lord alone. You shall love the Lord your God with all your heart, and with all your soul, and with all your might.
>
> *Deuteronomy 6:4–5*

and

> You shall love your neighbor as yourself.
>
> *Leviticus 19:18*

Whether or not the connection of these two commandments was already current in Judaism, Jesus joined them and emphatically placed the law of love before his followers, insisting that our loving brings a marvelous unity to our lives. He who came to reveal God's love to us tells us to respond to that love by loving: love God, love your neighbor, love yourself. That unity in our lives is further emphasized by John:

> Those who say, "I love God," and hate their brothers or sisters, are liars; for those who do not love a brother or sister whom they have seen, cannot love God whom they

have not seen. The commandment we have from him is this: those who love God must love their brothers and sisters also.

1 John 4:20–21

At the end of his life, Jesus gathered for a meal, the last of many, some of those who were closest to him. During that meal he spoke about what he had been demonstrating:

"This is my commandment, that you love one another as I have loved you. No one has greater love than this, to lay down one's life for one's friends. You are my friends if you do what I command you. I do not call you servants any longer, because the servant does not know what the master is doing; but I have called you friends, because I have made known to you everything that I have heard from my Father."

John 15:12–15

In other words, Jesus said, "Always remember me as your friend. Think of the things I did and the things I said as demonstrations of friendship. Realize how close I have been to you. Notice that I have made your joys and heartaches my own. I have been present to you in your fears and in your laughter. I have spilled out my heart to you and told you everything God has told me. I have let you experience my frustrations and my pain. I have been a friend to you and have invited you to be friends with me. I want you to be friends with my God. And I want you to be friends with each other." Having already knelt down and washed our feet, and soon to stretch out his arms on the cross, Jesus proved how much God loves us. Jesus, the tremendous lover, is truly our friend.

Befriending

It is helpful to see Christian life then as a process of being befriended and of befriending. God takes the initiative in loving and

befriends us by sending the only Son. Jesus spends his life revealing
to us the nature of God's love and calls us his friends. He teaches us
how to love God, how to love neighbor, and how to love self—how to
be friends with God, how to be friends with neighbor, how to be
friends with ourselves, how to *befriend*.

Being befriended provides us a magnificent experience of God's
grace and of the graciousness of God's ways with us. It is an enterprise at the heart of the gospel, of God's revelation of self to us. For
us to take seriously the fact of God's grace can make the difference
between a life focused on self, one of self-absorption, and a life
focused on God, one of preoccupation with God and God's love.
Those are the choices.

Rather than choosing to live as though we need to save ourselves, we choose to live like those who have been saved and are being
saved. Rather than spending our lives worrying about *our* energy, *our*
effort, *our* loving, we learn to bask in *Jesus' love* as we bask in the
sunshine. We allow Jesus to befriend us.

And so we come face-to-face with that truth which is both the
most consoling and the most difficult for us to appreciate:

> In this is love,
> not that we loved God,
> but that God loved us
> and sent his Son
> to be the atoning sacrifice for our sins.
> *1 John 4:10*

There may be no gospel teaching more timely for the contemporary Christian: *God loved us first!* We spend our lives trying to fathom
this truth and to accept it. Often we are haunted with the idea that
somehow we should be saving ourselves, making ourselves holy. For
many of us it may take years of trying and failing at this before it
finally dawns on us that saving ourselves does not work. It isn't supposed to work, because it is a reversal of the way of love. God does
not, somehow, look out at all who are already good and lovely and

dedicated and then name them "holy." We are good and lovely and dedicated because God has loved us and we have had the grace to respond to that love. We spend our lives responding to love, living "in answer" to a greater love that calls to us.

Everything, then, is grace. Everything is a gift. To the extent that we recognize and celebrate God's gracious love will we be able to respond to God's call and to be gracious both to ourselves and to our neighbors, the other friends of Jesus.

When we fail to celebrate grace and graciousness, we become *tough*. The pressures of life make us tough with ourselves, and we become tough with each other. Look around you at those who are hard on other people and you will find those who are hard on themselves. When we fail to celebrate grace and graciousness, we become *distant*—distant from ourselves, distant from God and distant from our neighbor. Look around you at those who are aloof and you will find people who are in some real way aloof from themselves.

In the incarnation, the mystery of God's love became flesh. That love became tangible and visible and believable in Jesus, who came to put an end to all distance. We who believe in Jesus, then, must put an end to all distance. We want to be present the way Jesus was, attuned to people as he was, and fully present to God after his example. We want to stop "postponing our presence," stop delaying being fully there with God, with self, with neighbor.

We have a tradition of honoring the "real presence" of Jesus in the word and the eucharist. Do we appreciate fully enough the real presence of Jesus to himself, to his God, and to his friends? Jesus did not live a "muffled" presence—the car muffler silences the sound of its exhaust system. Jesus did not live a "muted" presence—the mute softens the brilliance of the trumpet. We who follow Jesus dare not live the message of love in a muffled or muted fashion. If Jesus was *really* present, we who believe in Jesus must be *really* present, or the gospel will be sung by us only in hushed tones.

When the full impact of God's love grasps us, we want to live that love persuasively, the way Jesus did. Each day, then, we allow Jesus to *befriend* us, to embrace us and convince us of how much God loves us and how lovable we are—we allow Jesus to get our attention.

Think for a moment of one person in the gospels who was very enthusiastic about meeting Jesus:

> He entered Jericho and was passing through it. A man was there named Zacchaeus; he was a chief tax collector and was rich. He was trying to see who Jesus was, but on account of the crowd he could not, because he was short in stature. So he ran ahead and climbed a sycamore tree to see him, because he was going to pass that way. When Jesus came to the place, he looked up and said to him, "Zacchaeus, hurry and come down; for I must stay at your house today." So he hurried down and was happy to welcome him.
>
> *Luke 19:1–6*

Notice that Zacchaeus, before he met Jesus, already had the grace of wanting to meet him, "to see who Jesus was." He was so enthusiastic about meeting Jesus that he was willing to climb a tree. And he who was trying to see Jesus was seen *by* Jesus. Jesus invited himself to Zacchaeus' house, and to *stay!* We too spend our lives trying to catch a glimpse of Jesus, being interested in him and what he says, willing to "climb a tree" at times, always ready to respond quickly and to receive Jesus with joy. We spend our lives agreeing to be befriended by Jesus.

We allow Jesus to touch us in our gladness and to touch us in our sadness. We pour out our hearts to Jesus. We tell Jesus about the events of our day and ask him to help us through the days to follow. We allow Jesus to feed us, to nourish us in our hunger. We ask Jesus to be present to us in our celebrations and in our mourning. We invite Jesus to touch us with healing and to give us understanding in our confusions. We ask Jesus to send us the Holy Spirit to guide us in our choices. We ask Jesus to be our friend. Only then can we be friends with ourselves, with God, and with the other friends of Jesus.

MATERIAL FOR YOUR REFLECTION

1. *Sacred Scripture*

● Jesus said to him, "Today salvation has come to this house, because he too is a son of Abraham. For the Son of Man came to seek out and to save the lost."

Luke 19:9–10

● After he had washed their feet, had put on his robe, and had returned to the table, he said to them, "Do you know what I have done to you?"

John 13:12

● By grace you have been saved through faith, and this is not your own doing; it is the gift of God—not the result of works, so that no one may boast.

Ephesians 2:8–9

● . . . God's love has been poured into our hearts through the Holy Spirit that has been given to us. For while we were still weak, at the right time Christ died for the ungodly.

Romans 5:5–6

2. *Other Sources*

● . . . grace emerges only in the mutual opening-up of God and human beings. This interchange alters both: God becomes human and humanity becomes divine. The Incarnation is the prime expression of this mutual sympathy between the two: not only does God come to encounter humanity but humanity goes out continually to search for God. Jesus of Nazareth, God made human, represents the meeting of these two movements, the embrace of two loves that have been secretly searching for each other all the time. Of course the human search for God is the effect of God's

search for humanity. God created human beings in such a way that
they are always out looking for the Absolute. They are so structured in their innermost depths that real encounter with God
constitutes their utmost hominization and realization.
—Leonardo Boff, *Liberating Grace* (Maryknoll: Orbis Books,
   1979), 181.

● Jesus had a remarkable way of being a friend to every person he
met. We sense in him the ability to welcome the stranger, to find
the hidden gift in those called sinners, to strengthen the ability of
the loving to love more. . . . Those who could hear Jesus' message
left him with a greater love for themselves, with a clearer sense of
direction for their lives, and with a renewed awareness of God's
unfailing love.
—Paula Ripple, *Called to Be Friends* (Notre Dame: Ave Maria
   Press, 1980), 26–27.

3. *Moments of Retreat*

In your sacred space, read the fourth chapter of the first letter
of John. For a while, ponder verse 10: "In this is love, not that we
loved God, but that God loved us." Ask yourself: "Do I really believe
that? . . . Is the predominant tone of my life consistent with my belief
in God's love? . . . Do I celebrate God's gracious love in my life by
being gracious to myself?"

Think about Jesus washing the feet of his friends; think about
Jesus washing your feet. Are you reluctant to have Jesus wash your
feet? Are you reticent to have Jesus as your friend?

Imagine Jesus sitting across from you. Notice his regard for you.
As one whom he has befriended, tell him now what is in your heart.
Savor the rightness of communicating with Jesus this way, and find
an opportunity to do so regularly. Ask Jesus: "What do you think
about this, Jesus?" . . . "How do you feel about me, Jesus?" . . .
"How do you feel about my relationship with you, Jesus?" . . . "How
do you feel about my relationships with others?"

CHAPTER II

Befriending the Word

"Those who love me will keep my word"
JOHN 14:23

I have a boyhood memory of my father reading the bible. He used to do this regularly, perhaps daily, sometimes even on his lunch hour. One day I noticed that he hadn't placed a marker where he had just finished reading. I asked him about it, and he said, "Oh, I just remember a number. I might remember the number 822, for instance. I know that I'm in St. Luke's gospel, and next time the number 822 reminds me to start with the eighth chapter, verse 22."

Dad was an accountant, and I smiled then to realize how much his accountancy pervaded his life, even his faith-life. Looking back these many years, I smile now with even fuller awareness, realizing how familiar he was with God's word. He made God's word his home. When he was at home with us, he was at home with the word. In his own dwelling he dwelt in the word. He was familiar with God's word; he befriended it and allowed it to touch him. I think my father understood and experienced the importance of Jesus' words: "Those who love me will keep my word, and my Father will love them, and we will come to them and make our home with them" (John 14:23).

In today's rapid-paced world, dwelling in the word, being friends with the word, does not come easily. We are so used to reading for information, to being bombarded by print and electronic media, that we find it difficult to simply dwell with God's word. Rather than reading to gather data, we need to slow down and live with the word, mull it over, befriend the word. We need to reflect

19

anew on the word, ponder afresh its demands, and follow the path on which it leads us.

Why is this so difficult for us? There are many reasons. We don't find time, in the midst of our busy schedules. We feel inept, not trusting ourselves to understand what the word is really saying—we feel like a foreigner in a strange country so unlike our own, in times which are so different. We know that if we take the word seriously, we will need to change.

But God has the hope that we will indeed learn to take the word seriously and to welcome it:

> For as the rain and the snow come down from heaven, and do not return there until they have watered the earth, making it bring forth and sprout, giving seed to the sower and bread to the eater, *so shall my word be* that goes out from my mouth; it shall not return to me empty, but it shall accomplish that which I purpose, and succeed in the thing for which I sent it.
>
> *Isaiah 55:10–11*

So the word of God is meant to be a nourishing word, but it is a word that itself needs soil that is receptive and welcoming. To be truly life-giving, the word needs to be received by us who believe; the word needs to be cradled in our hearts, embraced in our lives, and allowed to touch us with its challenge.

Jesus is that word of God made flesh, God's word become visible and tangible:

> In the beginning was the Word, and the Word was with God, and the Word was God. He was in the beginning with God. All things came into being through him, and without him not one thing came into being. What has come into being in him was *life,* and the life was the *light* of all people. . . . To all who received him, who believed in his name, he gave power to become children of God. . . . And *the Word became flesh* and *lived* among us, and we have seen his

glory, the glory as of a father's only son, full of grace
and truth.

John 1:1–4,12,14

The word, the fullness of *life* and *light;* the tangible, visible Word
living among us—that is the word that the apostles proclaim:

> We declare to you what was from the beginning, what we
> have heard, what we have seen with our eyes, what we have
> looked at and touched with our hands, concerning the
> word of life—this life was revealed, and we have seen it and
> testify to it, and declare to you the eternal life that was with
> the Father and was revealed to us—we declare to you what
> we have seen and heard. . . .

1 John 1:1–3

The early friends of Jesus, then, proclaim to us the word, the
living word, the word they saw and heard—they proclaim Jesus to us,
the Jesus who calls us to be his friends and friends of his God. So we
need to become friends with the word, to develop an attitude of
receptivity to the word—an attitude of welcome. Henri Nouwen
writes that when we are hospitable, we create a "free space" which
our guest may enter.[1] Free space—a roomy space, a space that is not
cluttered, provided by a host who is available, ready to listen, gently
present, but who neither controls the conversation nor crowds the
guest with expectations.

So we "host" God's word. We try to be hospitable to it, to have a
welcoming heart, a listening heart, a heart that is truly accessible. We
put aside the clamor of the day and its preoccupations—Anne
Morrow Lindbergh's "caravan of complications"[2]—all those things
that have been demanding our attention. And we "pay" attention to
God's word—a term we use which is quite apt, since doing this does
"cost" us something. For a while we agree to be less absorbed with
ourselves and more absorbed with our God. We agree to be really
present to the living word, and to be touched anew.

The letter of James says it succinctly: ". . . welcome with meek-

ness the implanted word that has the power to save your souls"
(James 1:21). The word has been *implanted!* Jesus did speak of the
sower and the seed:

> A sower went out to sow . . . some fell into good soil, and
> when it grew, it produced a hundredfold. . . . The seed is
> the *word of God* . . . as for that in the good soil, these are the
> ones who, when they *hear* the word, *hold it fast* in an honest
> and good heart, and *bear fruit* with patient endurance.
>
> *Luke 8:5–15*

To *hear* the word of God, to *hold it fast,* and to *bear fruit* is no
easy task.

To hear: Railroad crossings have signs warning us to "stop—
look—and listen." Maybe all of us need to draw one of those signs
for ourselves to remind us to pay more attention to God's word:
really *stop* what we've been doing, *look* directly at God, and truly
listen—try to really *hear.* Then we meet God—we who have such a
hard time being present to others, and even to ourselves.

On a personal note, after my father's wake my mother asked me,
"Who was that priest who came from such a distance, but when he
was with me he kept looking over my shoulder at the pretty girls
around the room?" I knew immediately whom she meant. He was a
great guy who had, indeed, traveled many miles, and a fellow who has
a way of "not missing" anything. My mother, in the midst of her
sorrow, put it humorously—the "pretty girls" phrase—but she was
really complaining: "*He missed me!* He didn't meet me. He didn't pay
attention to me. He didn't really hear me. He wasn't fully present
to me."

In similar fashion, we have a way of "looking over God's
shoulder" when we pray the scriptures, a way of not really being
there, of not being fully present, of not listening, not hearing.

To hold fast the word of God: This is easy when the word is consoling and difficult when the word is disturbing. When we pay attention to the true demands of the word, we are stretched many times in

a direction we don't wish to be. We are confronted with the need to change, to be converted, to turn more directly to God. Our generosity is tested. A full embrace of the word means that our lives will be refashioned, our hearts reshaped, and in the midst of it all the image of Jesus will come to finer definition in us.

To bear fruit: When we allow our lives to be touched by God's word, we are called out of our complacency, and our lives stop being so cozy. Rather, the word beckons to us, summons us, calls us forth, and makes demands on us. There is a vitality present then, an ongoing growth and richness, and this becomes obvious in our lives—in our prayer, in our sense of self, and in our relationships; we are truly bearing fruit.

pg. 27

APPROACHING THE WORD

I. *God's Word in Personal Prayer*

If you do not have a recent edition of the bible, it would be helpful to obtain one with a translation with which you feel comfortable. Note the introductions to the various books, the footnotes throughout the text, and the cross-references provided. Also, realize that separate commentaries on the individual books of the Old and New Testaments are available, and that there are more extensive, all-embracing commentaries too, one of the more recent being the *New Jerome Biblical Commentary*.[3] The latter would be a great investment for an individual, a couple, a religious community, or a group of friends.

Introductions, footnotes, cross-references, and commentaries are merely means to our understanding the sacred text and feeling at home with it. As we begin, we ask for the guidance of the Holy Spirit. Then we turn, for instance, to the book of Ruth, to the gospel according to Luke, to the letter to the Ephesians—to personally meet God in the word, to be touched by the word, and changed.

Many authors have written books to help break open the word of God for us. They can help us with their suggestions; we can even allow them to become a kind of personal coach for us. For instance, one current text introduces us to the monastic tradition of *lectio*.[4] In chapter four of this text, the author, Thelma Hall, reminds us:

> . . . The Spirit whom Jesus promised the Father would send in his name to dwell within us is the same Spirit who vivifies the word of scripture. It is my active *faith* in this Spirit, present in the word *and* in me, which, when brought into the reading and hearing of scripture, "in-spires" or "breathes into" it the living reality of the Speaker.[5]

The author reminds us of the steps of a prayer which is rooted in the word: (1) *reading and listening to the word* (*lectio*) in which, after quieting our body and mind, we choose a short text and read it slowly, "listening to it interiorly with full attention"; (2) *reflecting on the word* (*meditatio*) in which we strive to meet God by knowing more about God and learning what God wants to reveal to us, by use of our intellect and imagination especially; (3) *the word touches the heart* (*oratio*) in which our hearts are open to God and gradually "the heart takes over in a simple pouring out of love and desire"; (4) *entering the silence "too deep for words"* (*contemplatio*), the prayer of interior silence.[6] I refer you to Thelma Hall's helpful text for a fuller explanation of these steps in prayer.

II. *God's Word in Liturgical Prayer*

When we pray the scriptural texts chosen for the liturgy, we join believers throughout the world in true solidarity—the lectionary readings are shared by many of the major denominations. It is important to remember that the liturgy embraces both the liturgy of the eucharist and the liturgy of the hours (formerly called the "divine office"), which is prayed throughout the rest of the day, with focus on the morning and the evening.

In the liturgy of the eucharist we are nourished at two tables: the table of the word of God and the table of the body of Christ. Just as we treat Christ's body and blood with reverence, so also we treat God's word with reverence. We do our best to "receive" both. The liturgy of the eucharist provides a systematic selection of readings of the word of God, a cycle spanning three years on Sundays and two years on weekdays. For our prayer at home, a missal of our own can be a real help; both weekday and Sunday missals are available. Before or after we have attended the eucharist it is helpful to pray the readings personally.

In the liturgy of the hours the church leads us through the book of Psalms once every four weeks. In addition, the office of readings presents God's word in an ordered fashion throughout the year, with companion readings from the saints. Each day in the various hours of prayer, selections of God's word are offered. Scripture appropriate for various liturgical seasons is provided, as are special readings for feast days. As an aid to personal prayer some people might be interested in purchasing the one-volume *Prayer of Christians* or even the four volumes of *The Liturgy of the Hours*.

III. *God's Word in Informal Group Prayer*

In addition to our personal prayer with the word and our praying of the liturgy of the church, we can pray with family, friends, or community in an enriching, creative fashion. Informal group prayer is a great hallmark of our age. For instance, a group might agree to meet regularly for scriptural prayer. They might select a leader in a variety of ways—a leader each year, or every three months, or one for each meeting. The leader might have a commentary or two, and be delegated to prepare a short introduction to the readings. The members would have their own particular translation of the bible. The gathering would include reading the word aloud, silent reflection upon the word proclaimed, and praying the word. For each meeting, people might focus upon a scripture theme, or upon a particular part of a gospel, e.g. the beatitudes in Matthew 5.

A variety of the above is a group to prepare and/or critique homilies; I find that preparing a homily can be an extremely prayer-

ful experience. A couple, a community or a family might meet prior
to each Sunday's mass, proclaim the word, sit in silence, and share
their prayerful response to the readings for that day. Or they could
agree to meet following the homily at liturgy, sharing what they
heard, what they wish they had heard, what they would have
preached if they had had the chance.

Groups already bonded (e.g. basic Christian communities in
third world countries, women, men, minority persons, wives and
husbands, local religious communities, students) can experience that
special energy and focus that their shared situation contributes to
their prayer and reflection. There is a grand gift provided for all
believers when they minister the word of God to each other.

In every situation, whether alone or with others in one of the
ways suggested, it is helpful if the word is proclaimed *aloud*. The
living word then has a better chance to be heard, appealing to our
ears as well as to our listening hearts.

Living the Word

A good part of the remainder of this text will focus on our living
of the word. For it is not enough to listen. We are called to be
touched by the word, called forth and sent forth by the word,
stretched by the demands of God's living word, unsettled by the need
to live out its implications in the ever-changing circumstances of
our lives.

Befriending the word means that we become very familiar with
the word and very alert to those places in our lives where it calls us to
change, to be converted, and to speak a consoling or challenging
word to others, either those up close or those afar. The great consolation is that we have the promise of the Spirit: "The Advocate, the
Holy Spirit, whom the Father will send in my name, will teach
you everything, and remind you of all that I have said to you"
(John 14:26).

Our call, then, is to *be reminded,* to live the kind of life wherein it
is possible for us to be mindful of God's word, calling it to mind
throughout our day, and reminding each other by word and example

how a contemporary believer can befriend the word in authentic ways.

MATERIAL FOR YOUR REFLECTION

1. *Sacred Scripture*

- The word of God is living and active, sharper than any two-edged sword, piercing until it divides soul from spirit, joints from marrow; it is able to judge the thoughts and intentions of the heart.

  Hebrews 4:12

- Let the word of Christ dwell in you richly; teach and admonish one another in all wisdom; and with gratitude in your hearts sing psalms, hymns, and spiritual songs to God.

  Colossians 3:16

- We also constantly give thanks to God for this, that when you received the word of God that you heard from us, you accepted it not as a human word but as what it really is, God's word, which is also at work in you believers.

  1 Thessalonians 2:13

- Be doers of the word, and not merely hearers who deceive themselves.

  James 1:22

- . . . you shine like stars in the world. It is by your holding fast to the word of life that I can boast on the day of Christ that I did not run in vain or labor in vain.

  Philippians 2:15–16

2. *Other Sources*

- The spouse of the incarnate Word, which is the Church, is taught by the Holy Spirit. She strives to reach day by day a more pro-

found understanding of the sacred Scriptures, in order to provide her children with food from the divine words.
—*Vatican Council II, Dogmatic Constitution on Divine Revelation,* n. 23 (Costello Publishing Company edition)

● Whenever the Church, gathered together by the Holy Spirit in a liturgical celebration, announces and proclaims God's word, it is aware that it is a new people in which the ancient covenant is perfected and made absolute. All of the faithful have been made messengers of God's word by baptism and confirmation in the Holy Spirit. Having been given the grace of hearing, they are to proclaim that word of God in the Church and in the world, at least by the example of their lives. The word of God which is proclaimed during the celebration of the divine mysteries is not concerned with the present, merely; it looks back also to the past and forward to the future, pointing to what should be so much the object of our hopes that in this changing world our hearts will be set on the source of true joy.
—*General Introduction to the Lectionary for Mass* (Second Edition), January, 1981, #7 (The Liturgical Press edition)

● It was the early Christians who first used the noun "gospel" or "good news" . . . as a way of referring to the content or message which Jesus proclaimed to the poor and the oppressed. We call something "news" when it tells of a new event, an event which has taken place recently or an event which we can now feel sure will take place in the near future. We say it is "good news" when the news is hopeful and encouraging, when it tends to make people happy. Good news for the poor would then mean news that is hopeful and encouraging to the poor.
—Albert Nolan, OP, *Jesus Before Christianity* (Maryknoll, NY: Orbis Books, 1978), 45.

3. *Moments of Retreat*

Identify for yourself some scripture passages of which you are particularly fond, ones about which you find yourself thinking. Study these passages, following the notes and the cross-references, and perhaps using a commentary. Prepare a short homily using some of these passages. Share this homily with someone. And as you continue to ponder God's word, stay on the watch for other themes that resound within you.

Are there some areas of scripture which unsettle or "jostle" you? Do you know why? In your journal, reflect upon the reasons.

Consider the possibility of praying the readings of the eucharistic liturgy each day. Get a list of the readings and give the practice a try. As you do this, jot down in your journal phrases that touch you and lead you to want to pray over them.

Imagine that you are going to start a scriptural prayer group. Write down some guidelines that you think would be helpful in focusing the meetings of the group.

Do a survey of one of the gospels, listing those verses which are particularly good news for you. Are there other verses that would be especially good news for the poor of the world? Continue the survey with them on your mind and in your heart.

NOTES

1. Henri J.M. Nouwen, *Reaching Out—The Three Movements of the Spiritual Life* (Garden City: Doubleday, 1975), 51.
2. Anne Morrow Lindbergh, *Gift From the Sea* (New York: Pantheon Books, 1955, 1975), 25.
3. *New Jerome Biblical Commentary* (Englewood Cliffs: Prentice-Hall, 1990).
4. Thelma Hall, R.C., *Too Deep for Words—Rediscovering Lectio Divina* (New York: Paulist Press, 1988).
5. Ibid., 36
6. Ibid., 36–56 passim.

CHAPTER III

Befriending God's Presence

"Oh that today you would listen
to his voice!"

PSALM 95:7

Some years ago the Ford Motor Company ran an ad: "The closer you look, the better we look." About the same time, AT&T had a similar one: "The more you hear, the better we sound." These slogans captured my attention. I began to think of them as they might apply to Christian life: "The closer you look at the world and its people, the more carefully you listen to the events of the day, the better you will grow in love of God and of those whom God loves." But looking closely and listening carefully don't come easily. The busy-ness of life can lessen the quality of our seeing and of our hearing.

Vincent de Couesnongle, former Master of the Order of Preachers, once wrote to the Dominicans with a special challenge in this regard. He said that Jesus always looked with love upon the people of his day, and that we, as followers of Jesus, were to continue the gaze of Jesus upon the crowds of today—we were to be *contemplatives on the street*. However, he said, it is impossible to be true contemplatives on the street unless we are *contemplatives in the room*. The street and the room, the room and the street. It is the continual rhythm between the two, the creative tension between them, that shapes the heart of the contemporary Christian. If we have too little quiet time in our room, we begin to miss the fuller picture of what is happening in the street. We see people, but don't see beyond their appearances; we hear the news, but never ask ourselves about its implications.

What is at stake, of course, is our call to befriend God's presence each day in every aspect of our lives—the quiet, thoughtful times in our "rooms," and the bustling, busy times on the "street." In this chapter we'll reflect on how to have a heightened awareness of God's presence and how to befriend it—thus growing in our awareness of God's love for us and others and of the opportunities for expressing our love for God.

Those who love God, of course, are meant to savor the meaning of life: "Mary treasured all these words and pondered them in her heart" (Luke 2:19). But savoring meaning, like looking closely and listening carefully, does not come easily either. The pace of life can be so hectic, the rhythm of the week so unbalanced, and there is often so little quiet and solitude. Let's stop, then, and look more closely at *pace, rhythm,* and *quiet and solitude.*

Pace

Thomas Merton is supposed to have said one time that Americans suffer from a peculiar disease—we feel guilty every time we slow down! Once I spoke to a group of young mothers about this comment. They agreed. One woman told of a recent exchange with her little son: "Johnny, what's *wrong* with you? You're just *sitting* there; you're not doing *anything!*" He answered, "I am too! I'm *resting!*"

When I was in my teens I experienced something similar. I worked at a local grocery store, a busy one with a long tradition of spoiling its customers. We even had a "call order" service: people phoned in their grocery order, our operator placed the order on a spindle, and one of us would pick up that list and walk around the store gathering the items ordered; then we would box the order and place it in the "call order department" where it would be picked up later. Much of the time there were lots of orders. Sometimes there were none. It might not surprise you to hear that even when things were slow, we call order clerks kept moving around the store, looking busy, acting as though something were happening! Don't we all sometimes keep moving when it might be better to simply stop and rest?

Certainly, many people work a grueling schedule just to get by. But others seem driven by the *need* to be busy—for the subtle honor that our society pays to those who are always on the move. Sometimes I think again of Burnham's old store and its shelf of cleaning materials—of the Old Dutch Cleanser woman, mop in the air, constantly moving in circles around the can! Be busy . . . keep moving! How do we befriend God's presence if we are always rushing? As a poster with a turtle on it has it: "There is more to life than quickening its pace!"

Working hard is necessary for most of us, but always moving at a hectic pace robs our life of "presence," of that kind of "being-there" that Jesus expected of his followers. Maybe that was his argument with Martha:

> Now as they went on their way, he entered a certain village, where a woman named Martha welcomed him into her home. She had a sister named Mary, who sat at the Lord's feet and listened to what he was saying. But Martha was distracted by her many tasks; so she came to him and asked, "Lord, do you not care that my sister has left me to do all the work by myself? Tell her then to help me." But the Lord answered her, "Martha, Martha, you are worried and distracted by many things; there is need of only one thing. Mary has chosen the better part, which will not be taken away from her."
>
> *Luke 10:38–42*

Jesus was saying, "Martha, I really appreciate your love for me; you serve me in such a tender, caring way. But you have not really *been* with me. Mary has—she's listened to me. I need you to be less anxious about *doing* something for me. I need you to take time out to speak with me."

If we are healthy and generous there is no end to the number of people we can serve, to the good things that we can do. The only answer is to follow the example of Jesus himself and to *leave some good things undone*. Some people never met Jesus because he was unavailable—he was with his friends at Bethany or down by the lake in communion with his God. Some people were never cured directly by Jesus because he needed to move on to other towns. One element of the incarnation, then, was the radical emptying that Jesus experienced by adjusting to the limits on his time and energy and to some of the other "incompletenesses" of the human situation.

The holy thing for us too, then, may be to leave some good things undone—so that other good things can be done. This means saying "no" to some chances to love so that we can say "yes" to other ways of loving. This means developing a lifestyle rooted not so much in a "no" as in a "yes"—a "yes" to listening to God in prayer, to pondering the marvel of God's presence in the world and befriending that presence, and to savoring the meaning of life. Agreeing sometimes to a slower pace and even to being motionless for a while enhances that possibility.

Rhythm

In the little book mentioned earlier Anne Morrow Lindbergh says that we often feel pulled in many different directions at the same time—an experience of *dis*-integration. She says that we need "the quiet, contemplative, drawing-together of the self"[1]—an experience of integration. In the midst of our business, our busy-ness, we need to develop a contemplative rhythm of life.

And in an early issue of *Envoy* Adrian Van Kaam wrote of the need to have in our lives a balance of "participation" and "recollection." *Participation:* work times, busy times, being-with times. *Recollection:* reflection times, slow times, alone times. (With care, of course, we can certainly "recollect" with others.) We need to recollect, *re*-collect, collect ourselves again, gather ourselves together. We need an integrating rhythm for our lives.

The rhythm that we work toward must be in keeping with our

lifestyle—monasteries have one rhythm, domestic households have another. The former, although often very busy, have a more regular rhythm; the latter, one which is much more flexible. The rhythm of our later years differs from that of the more energetic years, the rhythm when we are healthy from that when we are ill. The rhythm of life of the single person or the celibate differs from that of the married person and of the parent.

There is a daily rhythm, a weekly rhythm, and an overall rhythm of life. Often people will have a series of especially hectic days. With care they can "catch up" on a weekend, finding the time they need for rest and for some intellectual and spiritual nourishment. It is important to monitor the rhythm of our lives and to notice any negative patterns before we become overwrought. Living at the extreme pace of the workaholic is living dysfunctionally; it brings a kind of stress that can kill us and kill our relationships.

Some people seem to become overextended because they live beyond their means and so are always "behind" financially—extra jobs, less time with loved ones, working for those things that they can't find time to enjoy. Other people seem to be overextended because they approach tasks without a sense of what really matters. They can lavish time on that which may not deserve it. Not everything deserves to be done well; some things can be done "poorly," with a light touch. Weekly housecleaning is different from spring house-cleaning. Parents with little children may have to choose for the kids and allow the house to be a bit disheveled; better to put the house on hold than to be done in by trying to do the impossible and missing the little folks in the process.

My widowed mother, in her later years, used to come down the stairs after her morning shower, dusting the banister with her bath towel; and once she announced for my benefit: "Well, I've done my housework for the day!"—a nice sense of what was then important, finding some needed daily nourishment in her morning newspaper. And a pattern very different from that of her years as a busy nurse and then as a young wife and mother; but appropriate for her new situation.

Another instance from home: My folks had the practice of taking a ride through the Connecticut countryside every Thanksgiving morning. While they toured along, giving thanks together, the turkey roasted itself. When the company arrived, they were welcomed by two happy people, folks who, having already provided for their own enjoyment together, were able to pass on to their guests a truly warm welcome.

A life in which we are always working, always cleaning, always moving quickly can mean that we never fully *arrive* anywhere. We are fully present neither to ourselves, nor to our neighbor, nor to our God, nor to the world around us.

Quiet and Solitude

Times of quiet on a regular basis can help foster that interior silence that is at the heart of a healthy spiritual life. Sometimes things are unavoidably noisy around us, but other times we have simply chosen not to be quiet. We can be swamped with syllables, deluged by chatter, robbed of both exterior quiet and the quiet within us. For a moment, think of your day yesterday. Was there some quiet time? When you were in the car was it "all news all the time" on your radio? When you were at home was there the continual blare of television?

Even when we live alone or have some extended periods of time alone we do not necessarily experience solitude. It is possible for us to avoid true solitude by keeping ourselves very busy, very occupied, never having our days vacant enough to have room to befriend the presence of our God.

It is clear, of course, that a slower pace, a more balanced rhythm, a more quiet day with some solitude are not possible all the time. However, when we can moderate our pace, the rhythm of our days and weeks, the level of our quiet and solitude, we surely can be more fully present, befriending God's presence both in the silence and in the midst of our activities.

In a very real sense we are called to be contemplative all the time, we are called to a life of thoughtful presence. It has been said that there is one contemplation, with different moments, some in the more reflective times, some in the more active times. Let me address this matter a bit more fully by returning to the discussion of contemplation in the room and contemplation on the street.

Contemplation in the Room

We have already reflected upon our call to befriend God's word, to recognize its demands, to respond to its ongoing promptings. But God wants to be present to us sometimes without the means of a text, in an awesome experience of intimacy. I know of no one who writes about this as eloquently as does James Finley:

> The God-given metaphor of marital love provides a point of insight into the nature of our solitary intimacy with God and how it is experienced in the poverty of heartfelt prayer. The beloved stands before me as one who proclaims: "You and only you are the one I love. Only you in all of creation can fulfill my desires for fulfillment in love by accepting my love and loving me in return."
>
> In standing thus in the presence of the beloved I am in solitude first with respect to myself. That is, at the level of consciousness at which I perceive myself to be one among many I cannot grasp with my own mind my uniqueness in the beloved's eyes. For here, in this moment, I am awakened to the beloved calling me to realize *there simply are no others.* Unable to comprehend with my own mind this solitary uniqueness in which I stand alone, filling the horizon of the beloved's being, I am called by love to make an act of *faith.* I am called by the truth of the moment to accept in faith who the beloved calls me to be in love. By this act of faith I enter into my solitude in accepting my unique relationship of intimacy with the beloved in whose eyes I catch glimpses of a Self-in-love, which I cannot see but which I am asked simply to be.[2]

If we can bring ourselves into times of solitude we can simply be present in silence, calm and relaxed; sometimes it helps to notice the rhythm of our breathing, our inhaling and exhaling. We believe that

God dwells within us, and we retreat from images and strive to meet our God at the center of our being. One of the graces of our time is new interest in the practice of *centering prayer,* a "prayer of quiet." Much is written about it, but the basic prayer is very simple. Basil Pennington provides the following suggestions:

> RULE ONE: At the beginning of the prayer we take a minute or two to quiet down and then move in faith to God dwelling in our depths; and at the end of the prayer we take several minutes to come out, mentally praying the Our Father.

> RULE TWO: After resting for a bit in the center in faithfull love, we take up a single, simple word that expresses this response and begin to let it repeat itself within.

> RULE THREE: Whenever in the course of the prayer we become aware of anything else, we simply gently return to the prayer word.[3]

Our "word"? Perhaps "God," "Jesus," or "Love," or another that suggests itself. Whenever we find ourselves beginning to dwell upon any image or idea, we simply return to the word, repeating it silently. It is usually suggested that we pray in this centered, imageless fashion for twenty minutes or so at a time. Even a few minutes of this centering will usually bring an experience of feeling gathered, focused, attentive to our God who continually calls us to intimacy.

Contemplation on the Street

In addition to this *retreating* from images and concepts, we can also *turn* to images, to ideas and experiences, and reflect on them, dwelling upon their meaning. This is what I like to call the "open contemplative sense": a contemplation that is "open" to the wonder of an event, to the poignancy of a situation, to a glimpse of fuller meaning; and "open," too, to sharing the meaning we have found.

The impetus behind this kind of prayer comes from that challenge to each believer pointed out originally, I believe, by Paul Tillich: to live with the bible in one hand and *The New York Times* in the other. In other words, God's word is meant to measure, to critique, the events and decisions of this day, not only in our personal lives, but in the life of our nation and our world. So, as our eyes scan the headlines, the gospel echoes in our hearts. We listen to the radio news on the hour and watch the evening network television reports as *believers*—as people who regularly ponder God's word and its demands. And this makes a difference in our manner, in the quality of our reading, our listening, our watching.

This means, too, that as we read and watch we are thoughtful, full of thoughts. We recognize that which is consistent with the gospel and that which is not. As we listen, we hear that which is either consonant or dissonant with God's word. We are at peace with words that square with the word and ill-at-ease with those that do not.

William Callahan wrote some years ago about "noisy contemplation"[4] and helped me to realize that there is a way of attending to the media and to events that can make every day a reflective day, a contemplative day. In the midst of a busy day, we experience an event, overhear an exchange between others, or hear a bit of news from afar. When we are on the street we live with an awareness of that which is lasting, of that which has deeper meaning; we participate in the unfolding of history as persons who are fully there, savoring meaning, voicing opinions, shaping attitudes—we live with an "open contemplative sense." In the reflective exercises at the end of this section, I'll make some suggestions on how to develop this practice of open contemplation, of befriending God's presence.

MATERIAL FOR YOUR REFLECTION

1. *Sacred Scripture*

● Now more than ever the word about Jesus spread abroad; many crowds would gather to hear him and to be cured of their diseases. But he would withdraw to deserted places and pray.

Luke 5:15–16

- At daybreak he departed and went into a deserted place. And the crowds were looking for him; and when they reached him, they wanted to prevent him from leaving them. But he said to them, "I must proclaim the good news of the kingdom of God to the other cities also; for I was sent for this purpose." So he continued proclaiming the message in the synagogues of Judea.

  Luke 4:42–44

- But they did not understand what he said to them. Then he went down with them and came to Nazareth, and was obedient to them. His mother treasured all these things in her heart.

  Luke 2:50–51

- The master said to the slave, "Go out into the roads and lanes, and compel people to come in, so that my house may be filled. For I tell you, none of those who were invited will taste my dinner."

  Luke 14:23–24

2. *Other Sources*

- The balance of contemplation and action in the last twelve years of Catherine's life was not merely a relationship of complementarity. She did not pray simply to "refuel" herself for further activity . . . nor was prayer an oasis of rest from work, a kind of holy self-indulgence. It was precisely what she experienced in contemplation that impelled her into action. And all that she touched or was touched by in her activity was present in her prayer. Indeed, in her later years she was seldom physically alone when she prayed, except in her room at night. And her contemplation, on the other hand, was so present to her active life that she prayed and even burst into ecstasy within the text of many of her letters. This integration is the characteristic that marks Catherine among the mystics more than any striking quality of her mystical experience as such, and makes her writings so very pertinent today, when the

interplay between prayer and active ministry is so much at issue.
—Suzanne Noffke, OP, from the Introduction of her translation
of *The Dialogue of Catherine of Siena, OP* (New York: Paulist
Press, 1980), 8.

● In the silence of the countryside and the forest, in the cloistered
solitude of my monastery, I have discovered the whole Western
Hemisphere. Here I have been able, through the grace of God, to
explore the New World, without traveling from city to city, without flying over the Andes or the Amazon, stopping one day here,
two there, and then continuing on. Perhaps if I had traveled in
this manner, I should have seen nothing . . . generally those who
travel most see the least.
—Thomas Merton, as quoted by Michael Mott, *The Seven Mountains of Thomas Merton* (Boston: Houghton Mifflin, 1984), 314.

● Solitude is not entered into by way of subtle introspections. The
ego self does not transcend itself by its own efforts at self-
transcendence. Solitude is entered in the pure simplicity of divine
love. Perhaps with a great deal of emotional fervor or perhaps in a
dry-as-dust subtle stillness God awakens me to his love in a way
that is utterly personal and existential.
—James Finley, *The Awakening Call—Fostering Intimacy with God*
(Notre Dame: Ave Maria Press, 1984), 80.

3. *Moments of Retreat*

Some Reflections on the Media:
Radio news: Listen to *All Things Considered* on National Public
Radio (a total of an hour and a half in the late afternoon). Every day
you will hear voices of persons from near and far—some who are
celebrating a day filled with joy and others who are in the midst of
war or violence or starvation. Remember that Jesus came to save
those persons. Ask yourself if those around them and those who lead

them are treating them with the kind of attentiveness that Jesus would have shown them, the same kind of receptivity, the same kind of healing embrace.

Radio talk shows: Listen to *Talknet*—to Bruce Williams or Neil Meyers or Dr. Harvey Rubin. Notice the respectful attention that they pay to the wide range of people who call in, and listen to their responses. Wonder about the plight of those callers who seem overwhelmed by pressure. Ask yourself what Jesus would say to them.

Television news: Watch the *MacNeil-Lehrer Report*. Pay special attention to the *issues* upon which they focus. Allow your gospel awareness to be quickened. Make time to watch *Nightline* with Ted Koppel; dwell upon the presentation that evening, asking yourself what the gospel has to say to the persons interviewed.

Panel/audience participation shows: Try to find time someday to watch Phil Donahue or Oprah Winfrey or Geraldo Rivera. Notice that even in the midst of the sometimes sensational, real people tell their stories, and real people in the audience respond to them either in gracious or harsh fashion. Find yourself wondering about the story of all of their lives—their hurts, deprivations, joys and sadnesses. With the eyes of Jesus, look upon the wide range of persons you see. Ask yourself how Jesus would relate to them, what his manner would be.

Newspapers/magazines: As you read the reports, notice the tone of the presentation. Look carefully at the photos. Study the faces of people. Wonder about their situations. Look at the ads, and at what often, unintentionally, is a cruel juxtaposition: stories of deprivation beside ads for lavish material goods, reports of people being diminished beside ads for luxurious clothing.

As an example of what a contemplative reading of the news can bring to your attention, here are some things I've noticed in *The New York Times:*

- a photo essay on the Vietnam Memorial in Washington, of "the wall" of one hundred and forty panels of polished black granite bearing fifty-eight thousand, one hundred and seventy-five names (May 27, 1990)

- a photo of an Iranian mother grieving for her young daughter, who died in a devastating earthquake (June 23, 1990)

- a photo of a mass grave in Yugoslavia where people were murdered forty-five years ago . . . "the officers alternated who did the shooting so their guns would not overheat" (July 9, 1990)

- a report on Rio's 3,500,000 slum-dwellers (whose "favelas" or slums don't even appear on city maps); this adjoined a Saks ad for $17 men's hosiery "distinguished by the finest array of patterns and an unrivalled palette of colors, in surrounds that are both rich and refined . . ." and on the same page an ad for a woman's cashmere cardigan for $700 (May 15, 1990)

NOTES

1. Lindbergh, 53.
2. James Finley, *The Awakening Call—Fostering Intimacy with God* (Notre Dame: Ave Maria Press, 1984), 78.
3. M. Basil Pennington, OCSO, "Centering Prayer—Prayer of Quiet," in *Finding Grace at the Center* by Thomas Keating, OCSO, M. Basil Pennington, OCSO and Thomas E. Clarke, SJ (Still River: St. Bede Publications, 1978), 12–18, passim.
4. William Callahan, SJ, "Noisy Contemplation," in *The Wind Is Rising—Prayer Ways for Active People,* edited by William R. Callahan, SJ and Francine Cardman (Hyattsville: Quixote Center, 1978).

CHAPTER IV

Befriending Your Story

"The truth will make you free"
JOHN 8:32

Some years ago I was stationed at St. Joseph's Priory in Somerset, Ohio, where I was assistant to our director of novices. We had a farm, grew lots of corn, and raised beef cattle and chickens. One of my jobs was to deliver eggs to our customers in Zanesville. When I was there one afternoon, I stopped at St. Thomas School to chat with the Dominican Sisters who staffed it. As I went up the steps of the school I met one of the young students, a little girl with a book bag and a lunch box, obviously tired out after a hard day. I said, "Hi! How're you doin'?" Without hesitating, she said, "I'm OK, Father—but I'm not too swift in math. . . ."

"I'm *OK;* but I'm not too swift in math." I believe that she *was* OK, that she was *so OK* that she could spontaneously admit to me, a strange priest, the area in which she wasn't "too swift."

A few years later when I was visiting my brother's family my youngest niece, then a toddler, was sitting on my lap, and I said, "Lainey, you're a real sweetheart." Without hesitating, she said "I know!" I can still hear the inflection in her voice as she sang those words in her little-girl way. She *knew* she was a sweetheart . . . how grand!

I tell you about these little girls and how they felt about themselves because many of us who are "grown up" *don't* know we're "OK," *don't* feel like "sweethearts." Loving *ourselves* is, for many of us, the weak link in the chain of love. It seems that in our lives there

45

was so much emphasis placed on loving God and loving neighbor that the need to love ourselves simply got neglected. As we ponder the great commandment of love, then, it is extremely important for us to give due attention to the issue of our love of self. "Love your neighbor as yourself"—love your neighbor in the same way that you love yourself, love your neighbor with the same spontaneous joy with which you love yourself.

In this chapter, to emphasize the importance of self-esteem, I will focus on self-knowledge, self-acceptance, and our embrace of the truth of our life stories. In the next chapter, I will share some of the concrete personal ways of befriending our very selves. Following that, I will address the importance of befriending our call.

Self-Esteem

Whatever the reason, self-doubt, or lack of self-esteem, is endemic in our society, even in the lives of those who seem most self-confident. Often people develop a kind of swagger as a cover-up for the fact that they really are unsure of themselves. Whatever original sin is, lack of self-esteem must be one of the major effects of it. Some of us learn to marvel at the beauty of the world around us, but we often act like mere spectators, beholding a panorama of beauty everywhere our eyes can see, but never quite including ourselves. Maybe as we look out all around us on the grandeur of the world, we all need to take a few steps forward in order to make sure that we include ourselves!

Saint Augustine once wrote that people:

> . . . go abroad to wonder at the height of mountains, at the huge waves of the sea, at the long courses of the rivers, at the vast compass of the ocean, at the circular motion of the stars; and *they pass by themselves without wondering*.[1] (italics mine)

Not to wonder at our own loveliness, not to claim our own worth, upsets any attempt to live the commandment of love—for then we tend to see God as unloving and to relate to neighbor as unlovely. If we don't love ourselves we kid ourselves if we think that we love either God or neighbor the way they deserve to be loved.

People who see themselves as unlovable were in some very painful way never loved by others the way they needed to be loved; so they live somehow blind to God's creative love, blind to the power of God's grace, which made them lovable. They are blind to the grace which makes them graceful, grace-full. They seem unable to admit the fact of God's forgiveness, which reconciles them. So they relate as if to a God who is unloving, grace-less and unforgiving—they relate to a false God, a God other than the God that Jesus reveals to us. They fail to respond to God's call to friendship. They refuse to be befriended.

People who live with a faulty sense of self also spend their lives comparing themselves to their neighbor, identifying the splendid facets of others' lives but always feeling as though they fall short of such splendor themselves. They therefore shore up their own sense of self by trying to diminish others: they try to control others with manipulative behavior or to put them down with snide remarks. Or they stay distant from others so they themselves won't be compared unfavorably.

This can all happen in subtle and surprising ways. For instance, I believe that the craziness that people find in some of their ministers —control, put-downs or aloofness—is rooted in the fact, not always obvious, that many people in ministry feel terribly inept these days, both personally and professionally. So they, and all who feel unlovable, fail to love their neighbor the way their neighbor deserves to be loved. They fail to be friends with others because they have not yet become friends with themselves.

However, persons who are healthy emotionally and spiritually are so aware of God's gracious love and of the love of others that they are able to be gracious with and loving toward themselves. But how do we come to love ourselves? A wholesome love of self demands a capacity for: (1) self-knowledge; (2) self-acceptance; (3) embracing the truth of one's story.

1. *Self-Knowledge*

Self-knowledge, knowing ourselves, brings to us believers the awareness that we are God's beloved children. A clear sense of all that this implies is terribly important if we are truly to love ourselves. The Dominican saint, Catherine of Siena, a doctor of the church, understood this well—the call to self-knowledge appears over and over in her *Dialogue*[2] in which God speaks to her and she to God:

> You cannot arrive at virtue except through knowing yourself and knowing me (p. 88).

> . . . To attain charity you must dwell constantly in the cell of self-knowledge. For in knowing yourself you will come to know my mercy in the blood of my only-begotten Son, thus drawing my divine charity to yourself with your love (p. 118).

> . . . I withdraw my presence from you so that you will shut yourself up in the house of self-knowledge and knowledge of me (p. 123).

> The soul, then, should season her self-knowledge with knowledge of my goodness, and her knowledge of me with self-knowledge (p. 125).

> Self-knowledge alone is not enough: it must be seasoned by and joined with knowledge of me within you (p. 158).

> Be careful never to leave the cell of self-knowledge, but in this cell guard and spend the treasure I have given you (p. 363).

Catherine, in response to God's words to her, responds passionately: "With unimaginable love you looked upon your creatures within your very self, and *you fell in love with us*" (p. 49). "You, deep well of charity, *it seems you are so madly in love with your creatures that you could not live without us!*" (p. 63). (italics mine)

When we consider ourselves, then, as so loved by God, a God

who fell in love with us, a God madly in love with us, a God who can't live without us, it begins to *dawn* on us that we had better love ourselves. The dawn occurs every morning. Every morning, then, knowing ourselves better and more aware than the day before of the depth and constancy of God's love for us, we agree: we are lovable.

2. *Self-Acceptance*

As we come to know ourselves, we need to accept ourselves. Acceptance of ourselves as lovable is necessary if we are to be loving toward others—self-donation presupposes self-possession. The giving of ourselves to others in healthy fashion depends on our having a coherent sense of self. Only if I have a healthy level of self-possession can I turn to you, my friend, in a peaceful and life-giving way. If I am unsure of myself, I relate to you in less than mature fashion. In some way, subtle or not, I begin to bolster my sense of self at your expense.

Some people seem to be so unconvinced of their own lovableness that they spend their lives in a radically self-centered way. Their conversation focuses on what *they* did, where *they* have been, whom *they* have met, what *they* have planned. It's as though the universe revolves around them. Healthy Christian life requires *other*-centeredness, our having a sense of self so secure that we can be forgetful of self and attentive to neighbor. We can give of ourselves, agree to be "taken," without losing our sense of who we are. We can die to ourselves without being diminished.

3. *Embracing the Truth of Our Story*

Understanding, "standing under" our life story is at the heart of love of self. All of us have had heartaches that have been terribly painful and need to be acknowledged. Most of us have happy memories that deserve to be celebrated. All of us have gifts that deserve to be honored.

Some of us, in our early years at home and/or in school, learned that we were not to inflate ourselves—we were to be "humble." (Our mother used to remind my brother and me that one of the things a mother needed to do at times was to "prick the balloon" of her child!) That may indeed have its place, but if our balloons are forever being pricked and we never experience affirmation and convincing love from our parents, we grow up with a diminished sense of self, and this can hobble us throughout life.

We may have picked up the idea that humility meant admitting our weaknesses but not celebrating our strengths. An adult living of humility means, of course, embracing whatever is *true,* gifts along with foibles. The gifts are truly *gifts,* something we have received free. So we are not the source of our gifts—but we really did receive them. To spontaneously admit our gifts and to accept whatever affirmation comes is part of humility. When applause comes, we simply render an interior hymn of praise to God, the giver of all gifts, and thus there is no pride, no claim that we are the source of what we have been given.

The letter to the Ephesians sums it up rather nicely:

> By grace you have been saved through faith, and this is not your own doing; it is the gift of God—not the result of works, so that no one may boast. For we are what God has made us, created in Christ Jesus for good works, which God prepared beforehand to be our way of life.
>
> *Ephesians 2:8–10*

God's grace . . . God's gift . . . therefore no boasting. But also: God's *handiwork* (New American Bible), God's *work of art* (Jerusalem Bible) . . . created in Christ Jesus. Praise to Jesus, then, who "creates" us all along the way of life. On every page of the gospels Jesus can be seen engaged in this "creation" of people. Read through a gospel sometime and simply notice Jesus welcoming people and listening to their stories, Jesus clarifying, Jesus helping people to understand themselves. Jesus meets people who are confused and unsettled. After some time with him, people have come to fuller awareness and they are at peace. They inevitably feel good about themselves, because they have been met by Jesus; they understand themselves more fully, because Jesus has understood them.

As an example of this clarifying presence of Jesus in a person's life, read the fourth chapter of the gospel according to John, which tells of Jesus and the foreign woman at the well. Notice that Jesus was tired from his travels, and that it was noon, the hottest time of day. The woman approached the well, and Jesus asked her for a drink of water—it was Jesus who took the initiative. She quickly reminded him of the conventions, that he shouldn't be asking a foreigner for a drink—he would become ritually impure; and he shouldn't be speaking publicly with her. Jesus broke through the conventions and engaged the woman in a long, thoughtful conversation about the water he could give her, about the circumstances of her life, about her husbands. He gradually helped her to understand more fully the water he spoke of, the meaning of her life, and who he was. Finally she grasps the fuller truth, and this foreign woman becomes a pro-claimer of the good news:

> Then the woman left her water jar and went back to the city. She said to the people, "Come and see a man who told me everything I have ever done! He cannot be the Messiah, can he?" They left the city and were on their way to him.
>
> *John 4:28–30*

The woman, because of her honest conversation with Jesus and because of his tender presence to her and her story, came to an enhanced awareness of her personal truth. And so it is with us: as Jesus is present to us over the years we gradually come to an aware-ness of who we are and of who he is. And understanding ourselves more coherently we become bearers of good news to others.

It is important, then, for us to be thoughtful about our stories, and to gradually embrace the truth of our lives. Sometimes this means celebrating joys we have not yet fully appreciated; sometimes it means facing sadnesses we have been avoiding. Let us now look a bit more directly at the process of befriending our stories.

As a help to you in "owning" your own story, let me tell you just a bit about mine. Contemporary authors tell us how significant our grandparents are, so I'll start with those four persons, the parents of my parents. My father's mother came from Liverpool, his dad from

Stratford-on-Avon, Shakespeare country, where he was a house painter. They came to New York, then to Connecticut. This grandfather died of lead poisoning when my father was three years old. My mother's mother came from Cork, her father from Belfast; they were immigrants also, settling in Connecticut. Her father was an alcoholic, a "knight of the road," for which there is a Gaelic term. My mother was the youngest of nine children.

Liverpool/Stratford-on-Avon, Cork/Belfast. A grandfather who died young; a grandfather who was addicted—no stable presence of a father in either home, but two strong mothers. Even with that little bit of my story it's clear that neither of my parents experienced at home how mothers and fathers relate in healthy fashion to each other and to their children.

My parents were older when they married. After a year, I was born, and four years later, following two miscarriages, my brother Bob was born. With their two boys, our parents learned how to be parents "on the job." They learned very well indeed, and today I look back and marvel at some of the creative experiences they provided. We had a "*love bunch*": whenever any of the four of us wanted a hug, even during a meal, that one would simply yell out "*love bunch!*" and we would all get up, hug each other, and swing in a circle around the room.

We had car trips many summers, going to different places each time: Washington, D.C., Miami, Daytona Beach, New Orleans, Chicago, and Canada as the summers rolled by. In preparation for each trip there was a *till*—a coffee can on a shelf in the kitchen. Every Sunday night during the winter we would gather for a happy ceremony—putting money into the till. Mother would put in the money she had saved from the food budget that week; dad would empty the change from his pockets—there, perhaps, because we had all saved money by bringing bulk ice cream home instead of having sundaes at Peterson's dairy.

So ma and dad did many things well. But not everything. She was very explosive; her ready affection was balanced by a ready anger—shouts and yells and slaps. Dad was the nice guy who never got angry. We never heard, "Wait until your father gets home!" Some days we couldn't wait for our father to get home! In the years since they died I have gone through that process common to all members of families, I suppose: reinterpreting the family story—our home life, their relationship, and their parenting. I have thought about how I learned early on how to toe the line and how to be helpful. I have thought, too, about Bob's less compulsed toeing of the line and of the sometimes stern treatment because of this, and also of the joy and laughter in our house because of his readiness for fun.

I have come to recognize that our dad, because of his reluctance to be angry, left most of the corrections to mother, who took them on by his default. I have come to see that my mother was an "adult child" of an alcoholic—before anyone knew what that meant for her and for us. I could certainly go on, but you get the idea. Along with the joys and the amazing love that was present in our home, there was a certain amount of dysfunction.

My hope is that this autobiographical sharing will inspire you to reflect again on your own story. I believe that every one of us needs to ponder again how things were in our younger days and to muse over the lives of our siblings and of our parents and of their parents —what kind of childhood our parents may have had. Like me, when you do this you will better understand, probably finding some harshness, but also, it is hoped, some marvelous institutions like the "love bunch" and the "till."

The hope is, of course, that by looking again you will notice any spiral of toughness in your life, wonder about why it occurred, and do your best to break that cycle of craziness—for it tends to be multi-generational—handed on from one generation to the next. The hope is that you will notice again the patterns of grace, of affirmation, and of nourishment, and pass on more vibrantly the baton of graciousness. Multi-generational good news and generativity—any cycle of hardness broken, the spirals of gladness enhanced!

Contemporary Ways of Befriending Our Story

During my years as vocation director for our eastern Dominican province I attended many meetings with other vocation personnel.

Once at our national convention James Carroll, the author, spoke to us about our ministry. He said that we had a very privileged role—that of helping candidates to tell their stories. By the quality of our listening and by the questions we asked, he suggested, we could help clarify each person's story—maybe they would understand themselves more clearly than ever before.

One of the most helpful ways, then, to befriend our story is to *tell* our story, to listen to ourselves tell our story again, perhaps more clearly this time. By sharing our story with others who listen attentively and honor our story, we too begin to listen to it more attentively and to honor it more spontaneously. We explain things which are unclear, notice elements that are puzzling, and incorporate any feedback we receive into our next telling of the story. In between times we have the chance to "mull over" our story, to make it more fully our own, to "appropriate" it, to embrace it, to become friends with it in a fuller and deeper way.

We can share our story with a friend, a family member, a spouse, a member of our parish or religious community. We can appropriate our stories in more formal ways too: in spiritual direction, in counseling, in workshops attended with others having similar stories.

For some people the marvelous grace of owning their stories comes through twelve-step programs such as *Alcoholics Anonymous* and *Al-Anon*. All over the country, all over the world, every day and night, countless people find in "the program" the safe space where they can listen to the stories of others, hear the resonance with their own stories, and eventually, when the moment of grace comes, share their own story, having come to understand it more fully.

A man who has attended AA retreats regularly said to me one day, "Father, this disease is like a grace. The Program is a true blessing! How many places will you find a bunch of guys like this spending a weekend talking about the things that really matter and asking God for healing?"

People who have alcoholic family members or friends can attend *Al-Anon;* people who had or have alcoholic parents can go to *Adult Children of Alcoholics* (ACOA) meetings. They can come to recognize the dysfunction present in their families, the patterns they developed to "get by," and to change those ways of living that have been personally destructive or debilitating. Persons who suffer from other compulsions of their own or from those of others can similarly be helped—abused children, incest survivors, compulsive eaters or gamblers, battered wives or husbands, those addicted to narcotics.

Denial is the great enemy of befriending a harsh story—"If I don't think of that tough stuff it will go away. Why delve into all those things which hurt so much? If I keep them on the shelf they won't unsettle me. Hasn't my life been messed up enough already without giving more time and energy to that which has already done me in?"

When we are tempted to deny our story, Jesus says to all of us what he said to his first friends: "The *truth* will make you free." It's as though Jesus is saying, "For so long now, wanting to feel better, you have avoided some aspects of painful truth in your lives. But the harsh truth does not disappear on its own or evaporate like the morning dew—it needs to be *claimed*. Unclaimed, it goes underground, unattended, where it keeps gnawing away. *Tell* the truth to someone around you. Tell the truth to me. Tell that part of the truth you now recognize, and the deeper truth will emerge. When you are listened to by friend, by spouse, by a helper, by others who share a similar story, when you befriend your own story, harsh though it may be, you will become *free*. You will not be controlled by untruth anymore. And in the midst of your struggle to tell your story, others will be helped to tell theirs."

MATERIAL FOR YOUR REFLECTION

1. *Sacred Scripture*

● O Lord, you have searched me and known me.
You know when I sit down and when I rise up;
   you discern my thoughts from far away.

> You search out my path and my lying down,
>   and are acquainted with all my ways.
> Even before a word is on my tongue, O Lord,
>   you know it completely. . . .
> For it was you who formed my inward parts;
>   you knit me together in my mother's womb.
> I praise you, for I am fearfully and wonderfully made.
> Wonderful are your works; that I know very well.
>
> *Psalm 139:1–4, 13–14*

● Do not fear, for I have redeemed you; I have called you by name, you are mine. . . . You are precious in my sight, and honored, and I love you.

Isaiah 43:1, 4

● But now hear, O Jacob my servant, Israel whom I have chosen! Thus says the Lord who made you, who formed you in the womb and will help you: Do not fear, O Jacob my servant, Jeshurun whom I have chosen.

Isaiah 44:1–2

● You shall love your neighbor as yourself.

Matthew 22:39

● We are what he has made us, created in Christ Jesus for good works, which God prepared beforehand to be our way of life.

Ephesians 2:10

● Speaking the truth in love, we must grow up in every way into him who is the head, into Christ, from whom the whole body, joined and knit together by every ligament with which it is equipped, as each part is working properly, promotes the body's growth in building itself up in love.

Ephesians 4:15–16

2. *Other Sources*

- Our view of reality is like a map with which to negotiate the terrain of life. . . . Our route to reality is not easy. . . . The more effort we make to appreciate and perceive reality, the larger and more accurate our maps will be. . . . But many do not want to make this effort. . . . Only a relative and fortunate few continue until the moment of death exploring the mystery of reality, ever enlarging and refining and redefining their understanding of the world and what is true.

  . . . if our maps are to be accurate we have to continually revise them. . . . The process of making revisions, particularly major revisions, is painful, sometimes excruciatingly painful. . . . The painful effort required seems frightening, almost overwhelming. What we do more often than not is to ignore the new information. . . . Rather than try to change the map, an individual may try to destroy the new reality. Sadly, such a person may expend more energy ultimately in defending an outmoded view of the world than would have been required to revise and correct it in the first place.
  —M. Scott Peck, M.D., *The Road Less Traveled* (New York: Simon and Schuster, 1978), 44–46.

- A family blessing begins with *meaningful touching*. It continues with a *spoken message* of *high value*, a message that pictures a *special future* for the individual being blessed, and one that is based on an *active commitment* to see the blessing come to pass.
  —Gary Smalley and John Trent, Ph.D., *The Blessing* (Nashville: Thomas Nelson Publishers, 1986), 24.

- If only self-image knew how in the end spirituality would actually affirm it and infuse it with meaning rather than eradicate it, it would not be so defensive. . . . If only it knew that in sacrificing itself—even for a moment—its true essence could be bathed in unconditional love, it would gladly offer itself. . . . There is something in us that *does* know, something that *has* experienced unconditional love and knows that it continues to be available. Self-image does not want to remember this part. If only it did . . . if only it knew, it would not be so afraid.

—Gerald G. May, M.D., *Will & Spirit—A Contemplative Psychology* (San Francisco: Harper & Row, 1983), 125.

3. *Moments of Retreat*

Take a piece of paper and make an informal sketch of your family tree. Start as far back as you can, but definitely include your four grandparents. Spend some time reflecting on their lives, on the kind of life your parents may have had at home and on the situation in the world and church when they were youngsters.

Was there any ill-treatment in the lives of your parents? If so, do you see any possible connection between that and whatever harshness you experienced at home as a child? Reflect upon your relationship with your sisters and/or brothers. How did you feel about yourself relative to them during your early years? How do you feel about all of you now? If you were an only child, do you have any regrets?

In *The Meaning of Gifts*[3] Paul Tournier writes that as creatures we live in the presence of gifts all the time, and that as Christians, we have received the greatest gift of all, Jesus. Spend some quiet time reflecting on the gifts in your own life:

. . . the gift of life . . .

. . . the gift of your own person . . .

. . . the opportunities you have had that others perhaps have not had . . .

Take a piece of paper and make a "catalogue" of your gifts. Return to the list from time to time and add those other blessings which occur to you as the days pass.

Spend some time conversing with Jesus about your family tree and about your catalogue of gifts. Thank him for the gift of himself. Ask him to help you to understand your story more fully. Listen to him speak with you about the hurts of your life and about any incompleteness that you have experienced.

NOTES

1. St. Augustine, quoted by Dr. Paul Brand and Philip Yancey in *Fearfully and Wonderfully Made* (Grand Rapids: Zondervan Publishing House, 1980).
2. Suzanne Noffke, OP, trans. and introduction, *Catherine of Siena —The Dialogue* (New York: Paulist Press, 1980).
3. Paul Tournier, *The Meaning of Gifts,* trans. John S. Gilmour (Richmond: John Knox Press, 1966).

CHAPTER V

Befriending Yourself

"We are what he has made us,
created in Christ Jesus for good works"

EPHESIANS 2:10

After Thomas Cajetan Kelly was named archbishop of Louisville, but before he arrived in town, he was interviewed by a reporter from the local newspaper and asked, "What's the first thing you'll do after arriving in Louisville?" His answer: "I'll go and get my library card." I surmise that the unspoken conviction behind that statement was very sound, something like this: "If I'm to be a competent shepherd of the people here I need to be a person of ideas . . . a person who reads widely . . . a person who takes care of himself . . . a person who befriends himself."

Befriending ourselves does mean nourishing ourselves. And respecting and honoring ourselves. It means refusing to "do ourselves in" or to *be* "done in." It means refusing to live on the brink of exhaustion, refusing to treat ourselves like machines. When we fail to love ourselves, the outpouring of our love for God and neighbor is truncated, for then we love as those who are only *partially* present; we love in a manner much less compelling than both God and neighbor deserve.

Also, befriending ourselves means rejoicing in the gift of our sexuality. It means a lifetime of pondering the mystery of our sexual natures, of wondering at the marvel of God's design, and of gradually becoming friends with the whole person God means each one of us to be. It means trusting that our creator knew exactly what was being accomplished, that there was no huge mistake at the heart of who we are, but rather that our path to holiness specifically includes a lifetime of facing our sexual yearnings, confusions, desires and needs, and that in the process *we are prepared for heaven.* Jean Vanier, who has spent his life ministering to and learning from the disabled, has written with eloquent simplicity in this matter, saying:

> . . . if there is the discovery of being loved and believed in, that part of the heart which is most pure and innocent, and *which searches for communion* and celebration, will rise more quickly to the surface of consciousness.[1] (italics added).

Nourishing ourselves . . . honoring and respecting ourselves . . . rejoicing in our sexuality . . . being prepared for heaven . . . searching for communion—it should be clear, then, that in addition to befriending our personal story, loving ourselves demands that we *care* for ourselves, *take care* of and *befriend* our*selves*—an enterprise as much at the heart of the gospel as is our love for God and our love for neighbor: "Love your neighbor *as* you love your*self.*"

Let us, then, reflect on some of the ways we might love ourselves in an enhanced fashion: by befriending our bodies, our personalities, our emotions, our intellects, our spirits.

Befriending Your Body

SLEEP

In the *Personal Health* column of *The New York Times* Jane E. Brody reports some alarming statistics which affect traffic safety:

> Millions of Americans do not get enough sleep . . . they stay up late to socialize or watch television, and they rouse themselves with alarm clocks often hours before they would normally awaken. Then they use artificial stimulants, like caffeine, to mask their sleepiness during the day.[2]

The author says that this "chronic sleep debt" is like an "internal sleeping pill," and that when it is combined with the motion of driving on modern highways, the result is truly deadly:

> . . . more than one driver in five has fallen asleep at the wheel at least once; sleeping at the wheel is a central factor in 200,000 to 400,000 traffic accidents a year.[3]

Perhaps you have had the experience of nearly dozing off at the wheel. I have. For instance, late one night, heading back to our priory in Dover, Massachusetts, I noticed the I-95 road sign which signaled my exit. I drove the half mile to the exit, but then passed the ramp, and had to back up twenty feet to make my turn. Apparently I had nodded off.

Other times my lack of sufficient sleep has shown up in slightly more subtle ways: by my eyes closing momentarily while meeting with someone during a conference, or by sitting at my word processor and continually getting "beeped" because I am missing letters—when I'm rested, my fingers run along smoothly; when I'm tired, they don't—the level of my fatigue is monitored by the number of "beeps" I get.

I mention sleep deprivation and my personal anecdotes to make the point: it is possible to abuse our bodies by not getting sufficient sleep. Forgetting the good example of Jesus, who even slept in a boat when expert fishermen were at the helm, we may continually miss the sleep we need to live productive days without undue stress. In order to get some needed rest, I have had to learn to "sleep over" on some Saturday mornings, for instance (and even to retire earlier on some Friday nights, although that's much more difficult for me), and I have learned to take an occasional nap.

Stop for a moment and do an informal "sleep inventory" for yourself: during a typical day, do you ever find yourself nodding off? Do you usually fall into bed simply exhausted from the tasks of the day? When you awaken, do you always wish that you had another hour or two to sleep? You too may have a "chronic sleep debt."

The really bad news is that it doesn't make sense:

Sleep experts insist that the effort to squeeze ever more tasks into one's days and nights ultimately backfires. The person who invests in a full night's sleep, they say, will be more than recompensed in heightened productivity, creativity and focus.[4]

WEIGHT AND DIET

Most of us Americans live in a world of abundant food—supermarkets with shelves so loaded that the food nearly falls off into our carts; highways crowded with fast-food restaurants; early-bird specials at all sorts of restaurants; coupons, ads and incentives to buy food and to eat food. Every possible taste, shape, color and texture of food; every possible choice: fresh salmon from Alaska, kiwi fruit from New Zealand; every possible package: juice in boxes, corn in bags to pop in the microwave. A marvelous bounty, but also a potential hazard: both our bodies and our spirits can become bloated.

A recent book puts it bluntly: "Americans, gaining an average of one to two pounds a year from ages 20 to 50, are heavier than are the citizens of any other major nation."[5] It is rather obvious that our world of abundance makes it hard for many to exercise the restraint needed to keep fit. A casual survey of a typical gathering of people will usually find a good number of them who are significantly overweight. And this in a culture which continually pushes fad diets and crash programs for easy weight loss.

For those having a problem with weight and diet, it might be helpful to start a folder of clippings—the popular press frequently offers fine information and advice for maintaining proper weight and for planning simple nourishing meals. Or you might browse through the health-care section of your local library for a general book on maintaining your weight, on making your meals more nutritious and your life more healthful.

A helpful little book, *Fasting Rediscovered,*[6] makes the point that some of us believers may lack restraint in eating and drinking because we think too much about *dieting* and too little about *fasting.* The church has always known that there can be a positive connection between curbing our appetite and having our spirit soar. While both dieting and fasting require restraint, fasting adds the intention of having us identify with the suffering savior and also with the hungry and starving people of the world.

Some people find it helpful to have a weekly fast day, with one full meal, limited portions at the other meals, and no eating between meals. A friend of mine has a hefty breakfast and a substantial supper each day, but he skips lunch and rarely eats between meals, sometimes having a cup of tea instead. That kind of discipline is not easy for most of us, for it demands that we be willing *to feel hungry sometimes.* Think of this: *if we eat until we feel full, we have overeaten,* since it takes about twenty minutes for food to travel to our stomachs, and only then do we have the sensation of "fullness." So if our normal pattern is to keep eating until we feel full, we are in fact continually overeating.

Feeling even a bit "empty" sometimes could, of course, help draw us out of the isolation we may experience relative to the hurting people of the world. And it might help us to feel connected with our sisters and brothers in the poorer sections of our own area and with those throughout the world who never have enough food, who not even once in their lives have been able to buy from an overflowing shelf of food, and who always go to bed hungry.

EXERCISE

We need to realize that our level of physical activity is directly connected with our weight, our body tone, and our cardiac health. Several years ago during a routine health exam a doctor commented that I was quite "sedentary." I didn't like his saying that, but I realized that he was right—I did put in full days, but they usually involved very little physical activity. I *was,* alas, "sedentary"; I *felt* sedentary; I *looked* sedentary!

Sometime later I had the benefit of attending a sabbatical program for priests, the Vatican II Institute in Menlo Park, California. One of the unexpected opportunities it provided was an optional group workout three times weekly under the supervision of Mr. Don

Nava, one of the conditioning coaches of the San Francisco 49ers. Before long I was helped into a level of physical fitness I had long forgotten; that astounded me, and nudged me into a more vigorous lifestyle. The result was a simple practice: I began to walk energetically several times a week. That helped me to maintain my weight and to feel more alert and more "together." I fall back into my old ways, however, and I regularly need to monitor my schedule and to choose again to exercise. As I read reports of the sudden deaths of people my age and younger, I wonder if some of them got so caught up with the tasks of their lives that they failed to take time for themselves, especially for exercise.

Don't be afraid to follow good example. I am strengthened in my resolve to be faithful to exercise by the example of the two oldest men in my previous local community: Henry is eighty-three, walks in the woods each day, golfs regularly, and skis when the opportunity is present. Ceslaus, who is ninety-one, and continues to live his vigorous lifestyle, is always carrying big loads of stuff to the dumpster, and makes several trips daily back and forth to his fourth-floor rooms. It is no surprise, I believe, that both of these special brothers of mine are also vigorous in their conversations!

CLOTHING

Some years ago I began to notice that whenever I wore a particular deep blue shirt or a bright aqua sweater, others would often say to me, "Joe, you look great today!" I never "had my colors done" formally, but I did begin to notice that some colors enhance my appearance and others don't. The point is a simple one: while maintaining a simple lifestyle, we can make choices of a color and style of clothing which are both appropriate and attractive—a very meaningful enterprise for us who are made in the image and likeness of God, and called to be very much "at home" in our own bodies.

Befriending Your Personality

Perhaps in recent years you have listened to public radio's former hit show *Prairie Home Companion* or the newer *American Radio*

Company and heard Garrison Keillor tell of his mythical home town, Lake Wobegon? If so, you heard the ad for mythical sponsor "Powdermilk Biscuits . . . the biscuits that give shy people the power to get up in the morning." Gentle humor: a light touch suggesting that it's O.K. to be a "shy person."

Lots of folks, though, shy or not, *never feel O.K.* about themselves—they never really "make friends" with themselves, never feel comfortable with their unique personality. Among the grand gifts of our day are those theories of personality which can bring us insight into our personhood, our uniqueness—our shyness.

Two theories are especially helpful: The *Myers-Briggs Type Indicator* and the *Enneagram*. The only way to fully understand their teaching is to make one or more of the creative workshops available. Let me say just a few words about each, mentioning several texts which might be helpful in encouraging you to make the workshops, if you have not already done so.

1. *The Myers-Briggs Type Indicator*

Before making this workshop, participants take a standardized test which gives them their personality profile, telling them where they fall on the following scales:

extrovert-introvert
intuitive-sensate
feeling-thinking
perceiving-judging

There are sixteen possible combinations.[7] If one is an "ENFP," for instance, she or he is an extrovert/intuiter/feeler/perceiver. In extremely over-simplified terms, such persons might find that they are helped to come to clarity by speaking their thoughts aloud, have lots of "hunches" as they listen to others, honor their feelings when making choices, and need plenty of time in making decisions about anything important.

Other persons begin to understand their own personalities: their difficulty in putting their thoughts into words—that they frequently need more time than others do in order to think things out; their attention to lots of details, from threads on the floor to veins on leaves; their concern for the ideas and values, rather than the feelings, that govern their choices; and their desire to pin things down, to come to closure on issues.

Whatever one's personality, each of the types is good; none is better or more healthy than the other. They are simply different from each other. And in the differences lie both potential enrichment and potential challenges—in friendship, in community, in marriage, and at work.

Understanding and respecting one's unique personality is very helpful in prayer also.[8] As we begin to befriend ourselves and love that which we come to understand about ourselves, we can find that our love of both God and neighbor has been enhanced.

2. *The Enneagram*

The Enneagram theory was developed by the Sufi Moslems. It takes its name from the Greek word for "nine" (ennea) and teaches that there are nine basic types of personalities. Again, in very oversimplified terms: the theory tells us that when we are very young, in order to be accepted by those around us, each of us begins to form an idealized self, a self which will be accepted. Each of these idealizations is in a particular center of energy: the heart, the head, or the gut. The idealizations of the *heart* are: "I am helpful" (2); "I am efficient" (3); "I am special" (4). Those of the *head* are: "I am wise" (5); "I am obedient" (6); "I am fine" (7). Those of the *gut* are: "I am powerful" (8); "I am settled" (9); "I am right" (1).

Again, each personality type is equally good and healthy. The only problem comes when we live our lives in a driven, compulsive way, when our own type becomes exaggerated and extreme, so that our lives are really caricatures of our truer selves. The journey to health is in becoming converted to a balanced, wholesome life—in becoming our finer selves, our healthier selves. You might feel encouraged to make an Enneagram workshop if you investigated one of the general texts on Enneagram theory[9] or a book written by two former colleagues of mine on prayer styles particularly suited to your personality.[10] The key is self-knowledge, understanding ourselves, and accepting ourselves even as we strive each day to become our finer, truer self.

Befriending Your Emotions

Many of us find it hard to acknowledge that our emotions are *good,* that they are God-given, part of the "equipment" given to us by a creator God who is all-wise. We tend to feel at home with the "positive" emotions, and are at peace with ourselves and others when things are happy and tranquil. But we tend to be very ill-at-ease, uneasy, with those feelings which seem more negative to us.

Sometimes people with young children or with older parents accuse themselves of having been overly harsh, because they had become impatient or angry at times. When these people talk about what actually went on, it becomes obvious that the impatience and anger was rather healthy—and exactly what the young or old persons needed to help them have appropriate limits in their behavior.

It might be helpful for you to read one of the gospels to check out the emotions present in Jesus' life. If you read closely, and place yourself in the situation with Jesus, you will detect his wide range of feelings, expressed spontaneously: from fierce anger with Peter ("You Satan!") and the money-changers in the temple, to warmth and, I believe, smiles when he spoke with the woman at the well about her many husbands.

Never be cautious about sound psychology. One of the splendors of the gospels is that they clearly demonstrate that a healthy psyche and a strong spiritual life are quite compatible with each other. Many authors specialize in writing about the relationship of psychology and spirituality; Eugene C. Kennedy, Gerald G. May, and Henri Nouwen are among my favorites.

Befriending Your Intellect

STUDY

I know a number of wives and mothers in their thirties and forties who have returned to school. After many busy years of raising children they have touched in themselves the desire either to begin college studies or to return to studies left incomplete. Other people have started taking classes in preparation for roles in ministry. Universally, this study has been truly enriching for them: they have a new enthusiasm for life, a fuller awareness of their own gifts, a sense of purpose which is contagious.

Some women and men, then, might be able to do formal study —completing their secondary education, studying by way of a correspondence course, starting or completing a bachelor's degree at a local college, or starting a master's program or even a doctorate in a field which has always interested them.

LECTURES AND WORKSHOPS

Others of us might profit by attending lectures and/or workshops on topics of interest to us. Many cities abound with such programs. When we hear about a program which attracts us, we need to decide promptly whether or not to attend; we can miss many worthwhile experiences because we fail to "pin them down," fail to make them a real priority in our lives.

THE LIBRARY

Someone once described healthy Dominicans as those who might come upon a table covered with magazines, journals and books of all kinds, find there both something they had already seen and something that they didn't care to read, but also a couple of books or articles which really engaged them, and which they might start reading for a few moments even then. I think this description fits many people: all those having an enthusiasm for ideas, a healthy curiosity.

To befriend ourselves by staying alive to ideas, each of us might well take Archbishop Kelly's example: get our card and use our library. Over the years, in different locales, I've always had the benefit of both our priory library and the public library; together, they have brought much richness to my life. In the public library I have often chosen books not otherwise available to me, books that were different from those I normally read—perhaps a book of poetry by William Blake, a copy of the best plays of the previous year, a book on the Andes, or a collection of the stories of Flannery O'Connor—something, that is, that would be *nourishing* and personally enriching; a text that would "broaden my horizons," "stretch" me, and jostle me out of my too staid existence.

In these times of audio and video cassettes, many libraries now provide a marvelous range of possibilities. How about listening to William Buckley read his spy thriller, *Marco Polo If You Can,* or watching *The Barber of Seville* taped at the Met, or the PBS series on the human brain?

Befriending Your Spirit

A friend of mine has a private thesis that Jesus interrelated with two communities: the apostolic community, and the Bethany community of Martha, Mary and Lazarus. In the *apostolic* community there was little personal nourishment for Jesus; rather, there was lots of instruction, constant repetition of what he had previously said many times, ongoing clarification of the nature of the reign of God, some corrections, and much patience—all of which added to his fatigue and sapped his energy. In the *Bethany* community, those friends of Jesus welcomed him warmly into their home, fed him, chatted with him, showed concern about how he was doing, affirmed him—they provided a chance for Jesus to get "off stage." If the spontaneous give-and-take of his times at Bethany can be taken as a sign of friendship and familiarity, Jesus must have been there regularly. At Bethany, Jesus was befriended, and his spirit was refreshed.

STRESS

Modern life, with its rapid pace, its ongoing pressures and frustrations, can fill our lives with fatigue and stress. Books and workshops abound on how to recognize and prevent stress in our lives. One thing is certain: if we're not careful we can start living as though we're only "half there," in a kind of daze, on "automatic pilot," on "cruise control"—a faint shadow of our more healthy selves. For the believer, that kind of existence is simply not good enough; it might be unavoidable from time to time, but as a lifestyle it falls far short: "Love your neighbor *as you love yourself*." Push yourself as if you are a machine and you will start pushing your neighbors as though they are machines.

Abuse of self does lead to abuse of others. We can end up being for others far less than they need us to be. Some of the aberrations in the lives of public people in both civil and church life are, perhaps, more directly rooted in misguided attempts to find nourishment and to fight stress than they are in any particular malice.

VACATION

Taking a vacation need not mean a lavish trip to Acapulco or a cruise on the "Love Boat." It might mean something as simple as sleeping in a tent in a state park, or even attending to your regular round of activities while on a kind of "internal" vacation. Being even a few steps "away" from the ordinary pressures of the day can bring refreshment to our tired spirits. Even in a typical work week it might be possible, with a little creativity, to "vacate," to find a "vacancy" in our packed schedules.

My father, in addition to spending each winter studying the "triptiks" for the coming summer vacation, arranged (probably at my mother's instigation) for the four of us to attend the periodic film/lecture travel series at Bushnell Memorial Hall in Hartford— ah, to be transported to the far corners of the globe before going home to face one's homework!

Frequently, weekends, when anticipated creatively, can provide at least an *attitude* of vacation. While living in Washington, D.C. I often had neither the time nor the money to do anything dramatic on a weekend, but I would always buy my own copy of the Friday *Washington Post,* with its marvelous weekend *Calendar.* I would pore over it, circling the things that I would love to do: from attending free concerts of the Air Force Band, to plays at the *Hartke Theater* at Catholic University, to the double feature movies for $1.00 at the *Circle Theater.* Sometimes I actually went, but even when I stayed at home, this musing about the possibilities helped me to maintain a "vacation mindset."

TELEVISION

Without spending an inordinate amount of time watching television it is possible for us to derive a good deal of refreshment from it. We might leaf through a weekly program calendar and choose something which will be nourishing to watch—an occasional "special," a *National Geographic* report on the underwater forests of the Amazon, a finals tennis match from the U.S. Open. Different from the "couch potato" approach of watching TV continually, we can select programs which have special appeal. Identifying them ahead of time can afford the same benefit as planning a vacation: the joy of anticipating the nourishment that is so needed.

LAUGHTER AND PLAY

Partway through the Nixon years James Reston wrote a column headed: "How About a Little Laughter?" He said that life in our government had become much too grim. Life can, indeed, become pretty somber for all of us. Laughter and wholesome fun are signs that life is in balance. One of the great indications that a marriage, a family, or a religious community is healthy is its level of play. Ferrer, one of the men in my province, recently deceased, had a favorite virtue which the Greeks called *eutrapelia:* the ability to play and to have fun. Oh for some explosive *laughter,* some *frolic,* some *play* in the midst of our critical times!

Laughter, frolic and play don't always just "happen," of course.

Often someone has *been* playful or funny, has helped us to laugh. Maybe more of the time we can be that person—noticing the incongruities of life, preserving a "light touch" when things are overheavy, being childlike and open to the fun of the moment, both for ourselves and for the benefit of those around us.

Befriending our bodies, our personalities, our emotions, our intellects, our spirits, then, fosters the kind of love of our*selves* which makes us much more apt to love our God and our neighbor. Any neglect of appropriate love of ourselves can mean a diminished living of the commandment to love. Times are much too critical for that to happen.

MATERIAL FOR YOUR REFLECTION

1. *Sacred Scripture*

● Now Sarah said, "God has brought laughter for me; everyone who hears will laugh with me."

Genesis 21:6

● Before I formed you in the womb I knew you, and before you were born I consecrated you.

Jeremiah 1:5

● Come to me, all you that are weary and are carrying heavy burdens, and I will give you rest. Take my yoke upon you, and learn from me; for I am gentle and humble in heart, and you will find rest for your souls. For my yoke is easy, and my burden is light.

Matthew 11:28–30

● Jesus called for them and said, "Let the little children come to me, and do not stop them; for it is to such as these that the kingdom of God belongs. Truly I tell you, whoever does not receive the kingdom of God as a little child will never enter it."

Luke 18:16–17

● The apostles gathered around Jesus, and told him all that they had done and taught. He said to them, "Come away to a deserted place all by yourselves and rest a while." For many were coming and going, and they had no leisure even to eat.

Mark 6:30–31

● Martha was distracted by her many tasks; so she came to him and asked, "Lord, do you not care that my sister has left me to do all the work by myself? Tell her then to help me."

Luke 10:40

2. *Other Sources*

● The British still keep the old English word for rest days: "holiday." They don't do any better with them than we do, but their fondness for historic preservation at least keeps the skeletal word alive from a time when rest time was holy time, holy day. Accounts of medieval holy days show some unholy edges, but nonetheless there was a sense of full, playful, and shared celebration that assumed an underlying value to rest time: a special window into that divine radiance just beneath the workaday surface.
—Tilden Edwards, *Living Simply Through the Day—Spiritual Survival in a Complex Age* (New York: Paulist Press, 1977), 196.

● Dr. Paul Brand, a noted hand surgeon, spent eighteen years in India doing research on the disease of leprosy. In the marvelous book noted below he tells us of some of the wonders of our body:

> *cells:* Inside my human eye . . . are 107,000,000 cells. Seven million are cones . . . which give me the full band of color awareness, and because of them I can easily distinguish a thousand shades of color. The other hundred million are rods . . . and I can distinguish a spectrum of light so broad that the brightest light I perceive is a billion times brighter

than the dimmest. (p. 22) . . . up to one hundred million million cells form from a single fertilized ovum. (p. 26)

bones: In 1867 an engineer demonstrated that the arrangement of bone cells forms the lightest structure, made of least material, to support the body's weight. . . . As the only hard material in the body, bone possesses incredible strength. . . . Sometimes we press our bones together like a steel spring, as when a pole vaulter lands. Other times we nearly pull a bone apart, as when my arm lifts a heavy suitcase. . . . We walk some sixty-five thousand miles, or more than two and one half times around the world, in a lifetime. (p. 70)

skin: There is no organ like the skin. Averaging a mere nine pounds, it flexes and folds and crinkles around joints, facial crags, gnarled toes, and fleshy buttocks. . . . Intricate spot-welds fasten a leg's wrap, holding it tautly to the muscle layer; an elbow droops loosely. (p. 118) . . . A normal hand can distinguish between a smooth plane of glass and one etched with lines only 1/2500 of an inch thick. (p. 125)

muscles: Seventy separate muscles contribute to hand movements. I could fill a room with surgery manuals suggesting various ways to repair hands that have been injured. But in forty years of study I have never read a technique that has succeeded in improving a normal, healthy hand. (p. 163)

brain: There ten billion nerve cells and one hundred billion glia cells (which provide the biological batteries for brain activity) float in a jellied mass, sifting through information, storing memories, creating consciousness. (p. 188)
—Dr. Paul Brand and Philip Yancey, *Fearfully & Wonderfully Made—A Surgeon Looks at the Human and Spiritual Body* (Grand Rapids: Zondervan Publishing House, 1980).

● *How can I live with wholesome stress and avoid distress?* The *Wellness Letter* of the University of California, Berkeley, gives us an answer in one long but delightful sentence: "Certainly a good, old-fashioned thigh-slapper can be a real workout, raising body temperature about a half a degree, setting the whole cardiovascular system pulsating, throwing the abdominal, lumbar, internal intercostal, sub-costal, and transverse thoracic muscles into gear, rocking the glottis and larynx, rumbling up the windpipe, and banging against the trachea to emerge, finally, in a burst of mirth that sometimes issues from a person at a speed of 70 miles an hour, followed by muscle relaxation." That finding agrees with what Norman Cousins learned in the 1960s; namely, that ten minutes of belly laughter gave him two hours of pain-free sleep. . . . The safety valve of laughter has a way of releasing us to gladness and restoring normalcy.
—Donald E. Demaray, *Laughter, Joy and Healing* (Grand Rapids: Baker Book House, 1986), 28.

3. *Moments of Retreat*

Sit in silence for a while and reflect on yourself. Remind yourself that you are God's child, God's work of art, created in God's image. Ask yourself if you treat yourself in a way which is consistent with God's design. Do you give your body sufficient rest and exercise? Or do you tend to push yourself beyond healthy limits? If so, seek God's pardon and ask for the grace you need to change.

Have you thanked God recently for your unique personality? Do you frequently compare yourself unfavorably with others? Along with whatever limits you find in yourself, do you also notice and celebrate your gifts and strengths? Pause for a moment and in your own words tell God of your awe at how wonderfully you have been made.

Do you have sufficient time for reading? Do you now have something to read which you are really looking forward to completing? Have you recently attended a lecture or workshop of special interest to you? Is there a particular television program you are looking forward to seeing?

How much fun have you been having? Is there some playful activity in your life? How much do you laugh and help others to laugh?

NOTES

1. Jean Vanier, *Man and Woman He Made Them* (New York: Paulist Press, 1985), 38.
2. Jane E. Brody, "Personal Health," *The New York Times,* July 5, 1990, B7.
3. *Ibid.*
4. Natalie Angier, "Cheating on Sleep: Modern Life Turns America Into the Land of the Drowsy," *The New York Times,* May 15, 1990, C1.
5. John W. Farquhar, M.D., *The American Way of Life Need Not Be Hazardous to Your Health* (Reading: Addison-Wesley Publishing Company, Inc., 1987), 141.
6. Thomas Ryan, CSP, *Fasting Rediscovered—A Guide to Health and Wholeness for Your Body-Spirit* (New York: Paulist Press, 1981).
7. David Keirsey and Marilyn Bates, *Please Understand Me—Character & Temperament Types* (Del Mar: Prometheus Nemesis Book Company, 1984) (©Gnosology Books Ltd. 1984)
8. Chester P. Michael and Marie C. Norrisey, *Prayer and Temperament—Different Prayer Forms for Different Personality Types* (Charlottesville: The Open Door, Inc., 1984).
9. Maria Beesing, OP, Robert J. Nogosek, CSC, and Patrick H. O'Leary, SJ, *The Enneagram: A Journal of Self Discovery* (Denville: Dimension Books, 1984); Helen Palmer, *The Enneagram—Understanding Yourself and the Others in Your Life* (San Francisco: Harper and Row, 1988).
10. Barbara Metz, SND de N. and John Burchill, OP, *The Enneagram and Prayer—Discovering Our True Selves Before God* (Denville: Dimension Books, 1987).

CHAPTER VI

Befriending Your Call

"I have called you by name"
ISAIAH 43:1

When I was a teenager attending mass in St. Brigid's Church in Elmwood, Connecticut, I occasionally thought about becoming a priest. We had a wide variety of parish priests, and I liked them all: Father Kennedy, who taught us altar boys that the hottest part of the flame on the taper was on the *outside* of the flame, so that we were wasting the people's time if we held the *center* of the flame to the candles; Father O'Neill, who was young and handsome, and a less demanding director of the altar servers; Father McQueeney, who was very gentle in confession and a great sport about living with a fiery pastor; Father Brewer, the fiery pastor, who was probably a saint, but who fired me from counting the collection because I wanted to quit being an altar boy.

So I knew and admired some fine priests; and though I thought about being a priest, there was one thing I couldn't imagine doing as a priest: *preaching*. But after high school I went on to Providence College; and after four years of accounting, I applied to the Dominicans, the Order of Preachers! Now, thirty-six years later, the reluctant, scared teenager of times past has done a lot of preaching—the marvel of God's grace, the wonder of God's call! I have found that if we are to love both God and ourselves, each of us needs to ponder our own call and to befriend it.

Over the years I have learned that others before me had been reluctant to respond to God's call, reticent in answering:

THE PROPHET ISAIAH:

I said: "Woe is me! I am lost, for I am a man of unclean lips
. . . yet my eyes have seen the King, the Lord of hosts!" . . .
Then I heard the voice of the Lord saying, "Whom shall
I send, and who will go for us?" And I said, "Here am I;
send me!"

Isaiah 6:5, 8

THE PROPHET JEREMIAH:

Now the word of the Lord came to me saying, "Before I
formed you in the womb I knew you, and before you were
born I consecrated you; I appointed you a prophet to the
nations." Then I said, "Ah, Lord God! Truly I do not know
how to speak, for I am only a boy." But the Lord said to me,
"Do not say, 'I am only a boy'; for you shall go to all
to whom I send you, and you shall speak whatever I command you. . . ."

Jeremiah 1:4–7

The reluctant prophet with unclean lips, the reticent proclaimer
who is too young—perhaps in the awesome presence of God the only
appropriate response for any of us is to be hesitant at first. But then
we remember that Jesus has named us his friends, and has called us to
be friends with each other. To the extent that we remember that call
of Jesus we will be able always to respond, always both (1) to admit that
we have been called, and (2) to recognize our call as ongoing.

1. *Admitting That We Have Been Called*

For too long a time in our tradition a call, a vocation, was seen as
the prerogative of the "church-person," the religious or the priest.
Vatican II tried to correct that attitude:

It is quite clear that *all Christians in any state or walk of life
are called to the fullness of Christian life and to the perfection of
love,* and by this holiness a more human manner of life is

fostered also in earthly society. In order to reach this perfection the faithful should use the strength dealt out to
them by Christ's gift, so that, following in his footsteps and
conforming to his image, doing the will of God in everything, they may wholeheartedly devote themselves to the
glory of God and to the service of their neighbor.[1] (italics
mine)

Hopefully, we believers are coming to recognize and embrace
the fact that *we all are called:* called to live the gospel and called to
proclaim God's healing word, each in our own particular set of
circumstances.

2. *Recognizing Our Call as Ongoing*

The original perception we have of our call is just the beginning.
Isaiah and Jeremiah went on to experience both the exhilaration and
the frustration of being prophets. The Virgin Mary embraced the
total future when she said, "Let it be done to me," but only as the
years unfolded did she come to understand the full implications of
her response to God's call. There were both joys and heartaches
which she could not have anticipated. So she had to give herself again
and again to her ongoing call; every morning she had to repeat
her "fiat."

Edward Schillebeeckx has observed that if we think that when
God called Mary to be the mother of the savior she was given a little
program outlining all that was to follow, we rob Mary of her life of
faith. No, Mary was not able to "peek ahead" and find out exactly
what would occur; she had no intuitive vision of it all, at least in its
details. Rather, her ongoing call demanded a steady gift of herself, in
faith, to God's will unfolding. Now let us reflect upon some of the
aspects of our ongoing call from God. We are—

CALLED TO BE FAITHFUL

Our lives, like Mary's life, are also lives of faith, lives of learning
how to be faithful. When I entered the Dominican Order I had a

fairly vague awareness of what I was doing; I am still learning about both the happiness and the demands of celibate priesthood in ministry and in community. These many years after entering the order I now know much more about both—about what it takes to be faithful. When people marry they have only a glimpse of what they are choosing, of the person whom they are marrying. These many years after their marriage, my brother and his wife know much more about what it takes to be faithful spouses and parents than they could have known at the beginning.

Basically the pattern is the same for most of us: we move from the romance and enthusiasm of our early years to the less heady, more demanding, sometimes extremely arduous years during which we learn how to live out the implications of the commitments we made long before. The romance is essential, of course: each of us has to be "carried over the threshold" of our commitments, "swept off our feet" by the wonder of it all. Without romance in our hearts many of us would never have responded to our call in the first place. But the full reality of what we have chosen, the harsher side of life, eventually rushes in; we can avoid it for a while, but it is meant to face us, to get our attention, and to confront us with the need to live our call wholeheartedly.

Fidelity is not a static concept, merely living out what we originally promised. As demanding as that might be, we are called each day, not only once. And each day brings its own surprise demands, its own joys and heartaches, its own opportunities for loving. To be faithful is a very dynamic thing indeed: to agree to be called forth today, to be beckoned to by our God and by the needs of those around us, to be "stretched."

CALLED TO BE GENEROUS

During my years working with seminarians I came to realize that what we really needed were men with generous hearts. It was fine if they were able in studies, had a gift for preaching and a love for the religious life. But if they lacked generous hearts, the rest was far too little. What God's people needed were ministers who could really meet them and be called forth by their unanticipated needs and requests. What people hoped for were those who were adjustable enough to relax their own agendas long enough to truly listen. What people wanted were others who would agree to be drawn in ways other than they had expected.

Having a generous heart demands that poverty of spirit which allows radical self-emptying. Father Chevignard describes poor persons as those who "find themselves on my path, in such a way that I would have to take a byway in order to avoid them."[2] To really meet the poor, then, is to come upon others on the paths of our lives and to refuse to look away or to avoid them; it is to meet the other and to agree to be "taken," to be called forth in such a fashion that the one in need never realizes how much it costs.

We see this generosity and loving fidelity etched on the faces of widows and widowers, their dream truncated somewhere along the way by the death of the "other half of their soul" (Augustine's description of a friend). They face the incompleteness of the dream they embraced years before, but remain faithful to the memory of their loved one and open to the life still to be lived. The decision simply to go on living made by those who have lost their spouse is a powerful witness to the sacredness of our individual call. The same is true of those whose loved ones have had a debilitating illness or accident—wives and husbands giving faithful love to their ailing spouses, parents spending their lives being present to their sick child, daughters and sons caring for an aged or frail parent—generous fidelity in action.

Our call, then, comes again each morning—sometimes in the midst of another rush of gladness, sometimes in embracing another dose of sadness.

CALLED TO COMPASSION

This side of heaven, all symphonies go unfinished. Unless we have dreamed little, there is usually a gap between our dream and the reality of our lives. In other words, human life is a finite existence—there are limits to our joy; as we strive to accomplish our dreams, there are areas of radical incompleteness. Fullness of life and completion of our dreams comes only in heaven. During life, then, when we experience that incompleteness which can't go away, we need to embrace it. If we're lucky, we have friends who give us powerful witness in this regard. Let me tell you about two of mine.

Bryan is a man with cerebral palsy. In his mid-thirties now, for many years he has been dependent on others for his bodily care, his clothing and feeding, his transportation. He speaks with great difficulty. But he has a marvelous wit, a keen intellect, a retentive memory, a courageous heart. With lots of help from loved ones he graduated from law school, passed the bar, and has worked for his state office for the disabled.

Kathy is a woman in her forties who was in a serious accident the night of her high school graduation prom. She was left paralyzed and unable to speak. She has been cared for by her parents, and, since her dad's death, by her mother and a dedicated friend of the family. She has a marvelous sense of humor, an enthusiasm for life, a communicative spirit, and, again, a courageous heart. She writes *one-letter-at-a-time,* slowly moving one finger to spell out a steady flow of words on her ticker-tape word typer.

Bryan and Kathy, both disabled, have each learned to embrace a life which is only a shadow of the life which otherwise would have been. They and others who are disabled in one way or other are finding meaning in the midst of the incompleteness of their lives, of their dreams. Limited by circumstances beyond their control, they are living their call in valiant fashion. Although they have never met each other, Bryan and Kathy speak exactly the same language—the language of life, the language of compassion received and compassion shared.

Our call to compassion, too, is a call to find *meaning* in that which in some ways lacks meaning:

> Blessed be the God and Father of our Lord Jesus Christ, the Father of mercies and the God of all consolation, who consoles us in all our affliction, so that we may be able to console those who are in any affliction with the consolation with which we ourselves are consoled by God. For just as the sufferings of Christ are abundant for us, so also our

consolation is abundant through Christ. If we are being afflicted, it is for your consolation and salvation; if we are being consoled, it is for your consolation, which you experience when you patiently endure the same sufferings that we are also suffering. Our hope for you is unshaken; for we know that as you share in our sufferings, so also you share in our consolation.

2 Corinthians 1:3–7

In the midst of our suffering, then, Christ's encouragement and consolation flow into our lives. Since Jesus really suffered, we are able to accept consolation from him. We are able to be en-couraged, to have courage breathed into us by Jesus, because we know that he understands. And so, having been consoled and encouraged in the midst of our own suffering, we can speak a word of consolation to our neighbor—the springs of consolation flow from Jesus to us and from us to others. Our call to compassion demands, then, that we be thoughtful about our own sufferings, that we really admit them and befriend them—only then can we be ministers of compassion to others.

It is always difficult to embrace our suffering, but never so hard as when our suffering lacks all meaning, is simply filled with frustration. How can parents find meaning in the death of their toddler? I think back to the pediatric ward of The New York Hospital in the mid-60s, and a lovely little three-year-old named Elizabeth. Even though to the casual observer she was a healthy little girl, she was not. Her parents, who commuted from Connecticut, visited every day. Gradually Elizabeth got weaker and weaker, and one evening I got the call that she had died. When I arrived in her room, I found her mother and father kneeling at her crib, praying to her. Those loving parents and I have not stayed in touch over the years, but I just know that they have been able to touch the lives of other parents who have lost children, of parents who face meaningless suffering in their families, because they too faced lack of meaning in the death of Elizabeth. From the human point of view, a sad loss of a little girl; yet in God's mysterious way, consolation overflowing, also, including that of being present to other parents and other hurting people in the midst of their meaningless losses. And that is where the *meaning* occurs—in compassion, "com-passio": suffering-along-with.

Meaningless suffering tends to isolate us. The hope is that we will refuse to *remain* isolated, and eventually reach out with love to those around us who are also searching for meaning in the midst of their trials. And this happens: the bereft widow visits the shelter for orphans; the businessman separated from his wife cuddles unwanted newborn babies in the city hospital; the celibate person breaks through the loneliness of Sunday afternoons by visiting shut-ins; divorced persons offer a listening ear and an understanding heart to those whose marriages are filled with tension. Rather than isolation, connectedness. Rather than self-enclosed people, people able, because of their own suffering, to be present to the suffering of others.

In his inimitable way, Bishop Fulton Sheen one time addressed the call to compassion in this way: he said that if one wants to be a good nurse or doctor, she or he needs two things: (1) *a sense of humor* and (2) *an incision.*

Let me explain in my own words the meaning behind the bishop's remarks:

1. *A sense of humor:* Incongruity is the basis of all humor. The humorist has the special gift of perceiving things that are incongruous. For three decades Johnny Carson, in his monologue, regaled the nation each week night by juxtaposing remarks which did not fit together—they were incongruous, so he was funny, and the nation laughed. The more sensitively expressed the incongruity, the funnier the joke or anecdote.

Bishop Sheen said that nurses and doctors need that special "sense of humor," that gift of perception; they need to wonder about what God is accomplishing in the lives of their patients; they need to be sensitive to their patients' stories and ponder the meaning hidden there. But they need something else too:

2. *An incision:* Unless the members of the medical team have had an incision, an experience of pain, they had better keep quiet. For the patient will realize that they don't know what they're talking

about—they've never suffered, so they have no right to attempt to speak words of compassion.

As we "befriend our call," then, we look at the flow of the years, at the persons in our lives, at the circumstances which shaped us. We look at the opportunities which we had and at those we missed, but would like to have had. We reflect upon the people who touched our lives with love and those who hurt us or abandoned us, who left us.

We celebrate the happy moments, and we ponder our "incisions." Gradually we come to appreciate this marvelous good news: *any incision* will do! Our call to compassion does not demand that we have exactly the same incision or hurt as the person across from us. If we've experienced the death of a loved one, we know not only something about every death, but also something about every loss; if we've had serious surgery, we know not only the fear of every surgery, but also that of every other precarious situation.

To befriend our call means that we try to be attentive to the events of our lives, to those times that have shaped us. We look again at all that has been gift, and at all that has been burden. Our thoughtful response to the call of today depends on our full embrace of the calls of yesterday.

To befriend our call means that we look closely at the circumstances of our lives now and ask ourselves: "Am I being faithful to what I have already promised? To be truly faithful must I choose something else? Or someone else? Perhaps God calls me to that. Or must I choose again that which my life has become, and embrace that portion implicit in my original answer, poignant though that may be? And does the new embrace of my own call make possible now a fuller embrace of those around me? Are they now a part of my ongoing call?"

It is important for us to have a keen sense of the "seasons" of our lives, of the particular "time" in which we live, both personally and globally, communally: "For everything there is a season, and a time for every matter under heaven" (Ecclesiastes 3:1). We often ask each other, "What *time* is it?" To more adequately appreciate and befriend our ongoing call, we need to ponder the mystery of "*God's time*," and "tell" the time to each other, pondering in faith the meaning of what happens this day, this year, this decade, and do our best to honor this moment of grace and take seriously the call of today.

As this section draws to a close, I am reminded of one of the saints of our time, a person who experienced in his life a dramatic *call* to confront injustice in his native land—Archbishop Oscar Romero of El Salvador. He was called by the circumstances of his life, by the times in which he lived—by the violence visited upon his Salvadoran people—to change, to find himself anew. He was touched deeply by the need of his own time and place. Archbishop Romero befriended his call. May his witness and the witness of the host of other valiant believers of our time in his land and elsewhere help us to cherish our call today and respond to it with true vitality.

MATERIAL FOR YOUR REFLECTION

1. *Sacred Scripture*

●   For everything there is a season,
   and a time for every matter under heaven:
A time to be born, and a time to die;
   a time to plant, and a time to pluck up what is planted;
A time to kill, and a time to heal;
   a time to break down, and a time to build up;
A time to weep, and a time to laugh;
   a time to mourn, and a time to dance.
A time to throw away stones, and a time to gather stones
      together;
   a time to embrace, and a time to refrain from embracing;
A time to seek, and a time to lose;
   a time to keep, and a time to throw away.
A time to tear, and a time to sew;

a time to keep silence, and a time to speak.
A time to love, and a time to hate;
   a time for war, and a time for peace.

Ecclesiastes 3:1–8

● Paul, called to be an apostle of Christ Jesus by the will of God . . . to those who are sanctified in Christ Jesus, called to be saints, together with all those who in every place call on the name of our Lord Jesus Christ, both their Lord and ours. . . . He will strengthen you to the end, so that you may be blameless on the day of our Lord Jesus Christ. God is faithful; by him you were called into the fellowship of his Son, Jesus Christ our Lord.

1 Corinthians 1:1–2, 8–9

● The gifts and the calling of God are irrevocable.

Romans 11:29

● When Jesus turned and saw them following, he said to them, "What are you looking for?" They said to him, "Rabbi . . . where are you staying?" He said to them, "Come and see." They came and saw where he was staying, and they remained with him that day.

John 1:38–39

● As for that in the good soil, these are the ones who, when they hear the word, hold it fast in an honest and good heart, and bear fruit with patient endurance.

Luke 8:15

● . . . you rejoice, even if now for a little while you have had to suffer various trials, so that the genuineness of your faith—being more precious than gold that, though perishable, is tested by fire—may be found to result in praise and glory and honor when Jesus Christ is revealed.

1 Peter 1:6–7

● It was fitting that God, for whom and through whom all things exist, in bringing many children to glory, should make the pioneer of their salvation perfect through sufferings.

Hebrews 2:10

2. *Other Sources*

● For the Hebrew, to know the time was not a matter of knowing the date, it was a matter of knowing what kind of time it might be. Was it a time for tears or a time for laughter, a time for war or a time for peace? To misjudge the time in which one lived might prove to be disastrous. . . . Time was the quality or mood of events.

This concept of time is not as foreign to us as it may at first appear to be. We still speak of good times, bad times, hard times, modern times and war-time. We say that the time is ripe for something or that an enterprise has no future. . . . The great prophets of Israel had the task of telling the people *the meaning of the particular time in which they lived* . . . (Von Rad).
—Albert Nolan, OP, *Jesus Before Christianity* (Maryknoll: Orbis Books, 1978), 74–75.

● Romero was a man who wanted to stay away from politics. . . . He had never given any indication of an excessive identification with poor people. . . . But he felt a responsibility as a spiritual leader. He began to see for himself what his earlier years in the church had not shown him—that the people needed a church committed to them, not just to the wealthy classes. . . . He began to help his parishioners find out what had happened to relatives and friends who had been killed or "disappeared" in the political violence. He kept a tally; by the year of his death it was averaging more than 500 a week. Peasants came to his offices from all over El Salvador to ask for help finding a loved one who had vanished. Each Sunday he broadcast a sermon and read a list of names of missing people over a nationwide radio station. . . .
—Steve Kettmann, "Churchman to the Poor" in *The San Francisco Chronicle,* March 25, 1990.

3. *Moments of Retreat*

Pause for a while and think of a time when you made a significant choice regarding your life. At the time did you recognize that experience as a response to your call? In retrospect, does it now seem more like a call which you answered? Are you aware of any call now beckoning to you?

Is there any area of your life which you might choose once again, embracing your call, now with a fuller realization of all that it entails?

As you think over a painful experience you have had, do you see it as a participation in the suffering of Jesus? Can you let Jesus console you in the matter and heal your heart of any lingering hurt?

Are you a person of compassion? Do you believe that the sufferings of your life which tend to isolate you are meant rather to connect you with others who are suffering?

Is there any area of your life in which you are now called to be more generous? Can you accomplish this without feeling diminished?

Have you praised God recently for the ongoing call which has been yours, and asked God to give you a gracious heart in living it to the full?

NOTES

1. *Dogmatic Constitution on the Church,* Vatican II, Chapter Five, "The Call to Holiness," #40 (Costello Publishing Company edition).
2. B.-M. Chevignard, OP, *Gospel Spirituality* (New York: Sheed and Ward, 1965), 161.

CHAPTER VII

Befriending Your Neighbor

"Love your neighbor as yourself"
MATTHEW 19:19

In William Blake's poem, *The Little Black Boy,* a mother is sitting under a tree, her child on her lap; she kisses him, and, teaching him about life and about God, she says:

> Look on the rising sun: there God does live,
> And gives his light, and gives his heat away;
> And flowers and trees and beasts and men receive
> Comfort in morning, joy in the noonday.
>
> And *we are put on earth a little space,*
> *That we may learn to bear the beams of love* . . .[1]
> (Italics mine)

That lovely phrase has haunted me ever since I first heard it. For sure, relative to eternity, we are on earth for a *very* "little space"—"the days of our life are seventy years, or perhaps eighty, if we are strong" (Psalm 90:10)—and for believers the task truly is to "learn to bear the beams of love." Each of us is called into an ongoing relationship both with our God and with other human persons. Learning to be present to God can help us to be present to others; and relating well with others can suggest to us ways of relating to God—what is at stake in both, of course, is the quality of our presence.

In previous chapters we have reflected on God's befriending
initiative in sending us Jesus, and we have learned from Jesus both
how to be friends with him and his God, and how to be friends with
ourselves. In this chapter we will learn something about befriending
the other friends of Jesus, our neighbors who are *near* to us, physically and/or emotionally; in the next two chapters we'll reflect on the
call to love those friends of Jesus who are "afar" either geographically or in some other way—they are strangers—people who are now
at a distance from us.

Learning to love our neighbor is a vital aspect of bearing the
beams of love, for we are called to love our neighbor *as* we love
ourselves. Alert to the ongoing call to come to a more wholesome,
coherent sense of self and a healthier level of self-acceptance, we
now consider how to love our neighbor in a spontaneously affirming
fashion. If we had no neighbor we might kid ourselves into thinking
that we have become holy; our struggles in the give-and-take of relationships reminds us that we have not. If we had no neighbor our life
might become a kind of cozy haven. We who follow Jesus, however,
are not called to a life of coziness—we are called to be stretched by
the demands of loving.

Jesus and Relationships

It would be helpful to read through one of the gospels and to
notice the manner in which Jesus related to his friends. You will find
him always attentive to the persons with whom he is speaking, taking
them seriously and expecting them to relate honestly with him. You
will notice conversations with a variety of "tones"—that of thoughtful appreciation; timely instruction; endless clarification, sometimes
with more than a hint of exasperation, of what he had previously
said; and ready correction, sometimes with palpable anger, of behavior which was inconsistent.

Notice especially Jesus and Peter. And see that Jesus refused to
put Peter on "hold," refused to squelch his anger at Peter. Jesus
knew that the times were too critical for that, and that Peter's role

demanded that he get the good news "straight." So Jesus expected Peter to hang in there with him and to always "mix it up" in hearty, spontaneous conversation, the quality of which was to be quite worthy of both the savior and the prince of the apostles. If more of our relationships evidenced the honest give and take between Jesus and Peter, they would be much more robust and healthy.

Friendship

Perhaps you have seen the little 2″ × 3″ "Pass It On" card[2] with the message: "We must have courage, faith, and lunch together sometime soon!" That about says it: we are more able to be courageous and to have a strong faith if we can all-along-the-way look forward to being together with a friend sometime for lunch . . . or a bagel . . . or a laugh or a cry. Being a friend means being "at home" with someone—or more accurately, perhaps, being "at home" with ourselves when we're with someone. It means not having to weigh our words or measure our phrases, not having to parse our verbs or diagram our sentences before we say something. It means being able to "blurt things out," trusting the friend to understand, to supply whatever might be missing. Being a friend means having an ongoing chance to reveal to another our real selves—our ideas, our fears, our joys, our heartaches, our questions, our plans and hopes.

It's not always easy to develop a friendship, however. Often in the early stage of a relationship, one person is more enthusiastic about it than the other is, and this is not always obvious. As time passes, it becomes clear that the two persons have different expectations about the "pace" of the friendship—how quickly it is developing and the depth to which it is leading. Among the more painful experiences of life is that of wanting to be closer to someone than he or she wants us to be or not wanting to be as close as someone would like us to be.

One thing is certain: the more *mutual* a relationship is, the stronger that friendship is. Although it can be painful to do so, it is helpful to monitor a friendship from time to time and to notice the level of mutuality; this is a help both to the friends and to their relationship. A relationship which is really comfortable to two people is a gift beyond telling. Such a friendship can grow and grow, and evolve into something far beyond the expectations of either person. But this rarely happens without painful times in which the relationship is tested. Sometimes those moments come simply because two people are so different from each other. At first their differences were points of attraction, but as time passes and the two distinct persons start being themselves more spontaneously, their differences become sources of friction.

Consider an example from the world of nature: outside my window at our priory in Dover, I had a bird feeder filled with sunflower seeds. Its most frequent visitors were chickadees, nuthatches, and tufted titmice; these athletic little birds zoomed in from a neighboring oak tree, quickly took a seed, immediately flew back to the tree, held the seed between their claws, pecked at it and ate the seed; and all went very smoothly. But sometimes the purple finches came, and they were *different!* They jumped into the feeder, stayed there and opened the seeds between their beaks, and left a pile of empty husks behind; in other words, they "camped out" and then flew away and left a mess! It took me a while to realize how unsettling this was for the other birds, the "flitters." When the finches were there, they threw the others off their rhythm: now, before they swooped in, they needed to check ahead to see if the "campers" were there; and sometimes they had to zoom off after a too-close encounter. The point? All of these birds were just being themselves; but in their being who they were, the others needed to adjust to them.

The connection with loving our neighbor? Sometimes when friendship grows the differences between friends become more evident, and the experience of adjusting mutually to the other can be unsettling. Precisely here, of course, is a great gift of friendship: a friend helps to *stretch* us. Instead of going our customary merry way, we now need to adjust to another. Instead of setting our own agenda, we need to check out the agenda of another. Instead of being self-absorbed, caught in our preoccupations, we need to attune ourselves to the interests of the other.

It is extremely important for both persons in a relationship to be their best selves, their true selves. This demands a very healthy level of mutual honesty. If one of the friends is always adjusting to the other, the one doing the adjusting is compromised, as is the relationship. Any pattern of one or both friends failing to be honest with the other will eat away at the fabric of their relationship. A strong friendship, then, is one in which both persons are capable of "speaking the truth in love" (Ephesians 4:15). In contemporary terms, this might be called "Christian assertiveness." For example, when I'm "assertive" with you, my friend, I tell you how I feel when you kid me in a way which is too biting, and thus hurtful: "Harry, when you joke with me in public the way you just did, I feel put down . . . I feel diminished." I *don't* say, "You've always been that way . . . people who know you can't stand you because you're that way . . . and I've had it with you . . . get out of my life!" That would be "aggressive" behavior. If more people understood the distinction between assertiveness and aggressiveness, their relationships would be healthier and their friendships would be more likely to flourish.

Speaking the truth in love is a worthy lifetime practice for every adult Christian. But perhaps it is never more crucial than in Christian marriage. A while back, good friends of mine invited some business acquaintances to their home for dinner. Barry, a very loving husband with a normally gentle gift of humor, lofted a remark heard by Vera, his sparkling wife, as she was bringing something from the kitchen. The remark felt like a put-down to her, and after a momentary silence, she said, "Now that's something you and I will need to talk about when we're alone." Honest. Direct. Spontaneous. Assertive rather than aggressive. "Speaking the truth in love." A simple acknowledgement that her sense of self had been affected, and a quiet but strong assertion that she expected to talk about the matter, rather than let it go unattended, rather than put their relationship on "hold" as she smoldered in silence. Christian assertiveness.

Supportive Helping Relationships

When one person is being helped in an ongoing way by another (by a neighbor, a spiritual director, a colleague, a mentor), it can happen that the help is provided in such sensitive fashion that to the one being helped, it seems very much like friendship. That person may experience in the relationship a level of affirmation and attentive presence beyond that in any other of their relationships—it can seem more mutual than it really is. When this matter becomes clear to either person it is important for both persons to speak about the nature of their relationship, and to clarify where they stand in its regard. If they reflect together on how the relationship began and on what has transpired since, it may become clear that their focus has always been on the one being helped, that the person helping has not revealed himself or herself in similar fashion, and that the relationship, although comfortable and spontaneous, is not really mutual, is not a true friendship.

It can happen, of course, that as time passes a fuller level of mutual openness develops, bringing with it the possibility of real friendship. Daniel Levinson, for instance, has observed that the mentor is often a transitional figure in one's life.[3] When the need for mentoring passes, the mentor sometimes can become a friend. Should this begin to happen, the shift in the relationship needs to be clarified; leaving it unclear can cause a good deal of pain and confusion. One potential source of pain both for the helper and for the one who was being helped is this: although a lovely friendship has flowered, the help which was so significant may no longer be possible in the same way; the helper is no longer able to be sufficiently objective. And even though the two new friends rejoice in the gift of their friendship, both may also grieve a bit the loss of the helping relationship they had experienced.

Friendship in Particular Lifestyles

Depending on our lifestyles, friendship takes on different modalities and friends face different challenges. I would like now to note, quite selectively, just a few of the distinctive issues which we tend to face because of the context of our lives.

FRIENDSHIP IN MARRIAGE AND FAMILY

One time years ago I spent an enjoyable evening with a group of happily married couples. Toward the end of the evening, one of the wives who was a bit older than the others said to me, "Wasn't it wonderful what Stan said about Betty, that she was his best friend?" It was, indeed, wonderful; but it was sad for me to realize that the older woman and her husband apparently had not yet come to see themselves as best friends. My own folks were, in fact, best friends. In their later years I used to kid them about carrying on a conversation without finishing their sentences. It wasn't that either of them was interrupting—rather, they had grown to know each other so well that often each was able to anticipate what the other was thinking and was about to say!

I believe that the mystery of God's love made visible, of love incarnate, love enfleshed, is nowhere more tangible and convincing than in that kind of loving Christian marriage. The day to day sensitive presence to the same person, with the mutual adjustments that are necessary to make a go of it, is right at the heart of the gospel love which Jesus preached. The oneness in mind, heart and affections that can develop between spouses over the years is a wondrous thing to behold.

Our renewal center hosts regular weekends for Catholic Engaged Encounter, and when I was part of the team for the weekend, it was always marvelous for me to witness the extent to which young couples are caught up with each other. I always tried to say to them, "Make sure you *stay engaged!*" For one of the hazards of marriage is that the "being-caught-up-with-the-other" phenomenon which is present between engaged persons often fades somewhere along the way. It was never meant to stay at fever pitch, of course, but sometimes it seems to disappear almost entirely, with a terrible distance setting in. Two good people can start going their own way, professionally and/or socially; or they can become so over-dedicated to providing opportunities for their kids that they miss each other. It is important for married couples, then, to make their own relationship a priority, to agree to fashion a friendship that will always continue to grow.

One of the graces of my life has been my involvement in a way of life called "Teams of Our Lady," an international community of married persons who are committed to growth in their marriages. In various parts of the world these couples meet monthly in small groups with a view to deepening their marriage relationships. Among the more profound elements of Teams is the monthly "sit-down" between wife and husband—an in-depth talk about their relationship and about the more significant aspects of their life with each other. The impetus behind a project-thesis I wrote some years ago on "couple communication" was that I came to realize that these really loving couples often had a very difficult time having a fruitful sitdown.

At first it surprised me that in the midst of all the intimacies of married life, having a thoughtful talk with each other was such a challenge. But I came to realize that sharing one's deep feelings, one's needs, desires and concerns, is an exercise in vulnerability— when we share so deeply with another it is easy for the other person to hurt us. The hope is, of course, that in a loving marriage there will be such an atmosphere of trust and safety that this "unfurling" of one's self which is at the heart of married friendship will be experienced ever more deeply as the years pass.

It is a marvelous gift to a whole family when this takes place. When things are good between mom and dad, things tend to be good with their children. When things are *really* good between mom and dad, their children tend to flourish. On the other hand, when communication is poor or there are ongoing areas of conflict between their parents, life is tough for kids. So often a child is expected to grow up before her or his time because mom or dad needs to lean on the child for support—their partner is unavailable emotionally and/ or physically. I suppose that what we all need most as children is to grow up in a loving, trusting atmosphere where real joys are present and celebrated, and the disagreements and heartaches of life are faced in a fashion in which no one is put down, no one is diminished —the gospel in action. Vatican II, in fact, calls Christian life at home "the domestic church,"[4] since life is so holy there.

FRIENDSHIP IN RELIGIOUS COMMUNITY AND IN PRIESTHOOD

Many older priests and members of religious communities entered the seminary or novitiate when the emphasis was on keeping distance from each other and even from the people they were to serve. Apparently, since young people are often very possessive of others, even exclusive, so that they shut out potential friends by always being with a particular friend, the corrective insisted upon for that kind of inappropriate closeness was a strange kind of "appropriate distance." The result is that whole generations of sisters, brothers and priests were told, even in the name of the gospel, to avoid friendships, and some of them even succeeded in doing so.

A great problem in the rectory and in the religious community is, then, that life in the past was often quite impersonal. Sharing eventually began to take place regarding ministry and the concrete details of living together, but all too often nothing very personal was shared. One wonders how many people have left the religious life and priesthood because they needed more warmth, concern and affection from those with whom they lived. Rather than having "left," perhaps many persons never were "found." Some years ago, at the end of a retreat I had given, I received a note from one of the retreatants, a sister, who wrote: "How hard it is to stay in this place hearing the same people talk of the same inanities, when I'm dying to share myself with someone who really cares."

The task for people who live together in religious settings is similar to that of people in family settings: to really "show up," to really be present. The call is to risk sharing that which is of substance and of personal import; the call is to respond to the daily countless chances to share deeply. Only when this happens consistently in the rectory and religious house will priests and religious come to be more "at home" with each other and with themselves, and better able to enter into relationship with those they serve in ways which are less stereotyped, distant, and controlling.

FRIENDSHIP AMONG SINGLES, THE WIDOWED, THE SEPARATED
AND DIVORCED

Singles

Perhaps there is no call more challenging than the call to live a
dedicated single life. Single people live without a claim on a spouse
and often without a stable faith community. They too are called to be
radically other-centered, and countless single women and men dedicate themselves generously to those in need. The temptation, of
course, is to become self-enclosed, absorbed in one's own issues
only, unbothered by the daily demands of family or community life.
The call is to cultivate a range of friends which is mutually support-
ive, but also able to challenge, and to continually call forth that
generosity of heart so necessary for true fulfillment.

The Widow or Widower

Along with the loss of a husband or wife, widows and widowers
often lose also their circle of friends. It's as though the friends who
knew them as a couple now feel awkward relating to them without
their spouse. Apparently their friends recognize their pain, but feel
unable to alleviate it, and therefore tend to stay away. My mother, for
example, after dad's death, was amazed that the customary periodic
outings with his brothers and their wives came to a screeching halt.
She couldn't understand not being invited anymore; it was as if all
those happy times had taken place because of dad, and that there was
no interest in maintaining the relationship with her. Over the years,
as I have come to know a number of grieving spouses, I have experienced this phenomenon again and again. Perhaps it has always been
the same, and that is one reason why Jesus brought such sensitive
presence to widows. His example might prompt all of us to live in
similar fashion.

Separated and Divorced Persons

Much of what has been said above is equally true for persons
who are separated or divorced. Add to that, however, the factor of

guilt, that vague feeling often hovering over the separated or divorced, concerning their relationships which failed—"How did I fail? Others seem to think I failed." Also, an unsettling ambiguity can exist in the lives of those divorced and separated relative to friends who are confused about their status, future plans, and freedom or lack of it. Finally, in addition to everything else, they go on grieving the loss of their marriages; they too need to be befriended.

Being Alone and Being Together

Each person has a deep core of aloneness, an intimate part of himself or herself which can be shared by no other, neither a friend nor a spouse. There is a celibate dimension to each of our lives, an element which reminds us that we are, truly, radically *alone,* and that we need to face that aloneness and agree to the rightness of it. It is also true that at times each of us is *lonely*—one of the most painful aspects of being human. But in our loneliness we gradually come to realize that only God can meet us at the center of our being, enter that area not open to others, and help fill our emptiness; and we continually ask God to nourish us in our want and to meet us in our aloneness.

Yet simultaneously we are called to relationship with others, to reach out to those around us. The gift of our sexuality is at the heart of this reaching out—we find ourselves being attracted to others, wanting to be close to them, wanting to spend time with them. Some people reach out to each other for a lifetime—they marry and often raise a family. Others have no particular other person with whom they fashion a life, but they too are called to be equally generative, sources of life and nurturance for others.

One of the more unsettling experiences we can have, regardless of the context of our lives, is that of becoming infatuated with another person. We can meet persons who are attractive to us, feel drawn to them, and find ourselves thinking a lot about them after we're apart. It's as though our hearts, heedless of the context of our lives and of our commitments, "soar" to the other person. Thomas

Tyrrell has written a helpful book, *Urgent Longings*[5] (a phrase from St. John of the Cross), in which he explains that just as our heart has the capacity to soar to another human person, so does our heart have the capacity to soar to God. In other words, we have only one heart, a heart which has a wondrous capacity for love. It yearns to love both neighbor and God. And in relationship to each it is shaped and fashioned, made over into the image of the Son of God, the Sacred Heart.

Fidelity and Relationships

Being "true" to our friends is an exercise in fidelity, in being faithful. A friend knows our gifts and our foibles, our strengths and our weaknesses, the gracious ways which are second nature to us and the harshness which is still all too prevalent. When our friends help us by being honest with us, by reminding us of the promises we have already made, they help us to remain faithful.

Friendship between men and women, especially, will be kept honest and true if they always regard the other in the exact context of the other's life, that is, not separate from the circumstances that surround them, from the commitments already made. If both persons are married to another, that fact demands a special level of sensitive mutual restraint which will help keep both faithful to their own spouses, to the promises already made. If the friends are both celibate persons, honoring the fact of their individual promises will help keep them from closing in upon themselves, or from falling into a pattern of expression inappropriate to their celibate lives—that which a friend of mine has called a kind of "magnificent imitation of marriage." If one person is widowed or divorced or single and the other is not, the latter should always try to remain aware of the special level of vulnerability that may be present in the life of their friend.

Fidelity is promoted as friends continue to commit themselves to ongoing growth. One with a generous and secure heart wishes that the friend will expand, will keep growing. It might be more comfortable if our friends do not change or "unfold," but if they do, it is a tribute to our love for them and potentially a marvelous source of richness for our relationships.

Reconciliation and Forgiveness

Whenever people are close to each other they will sometimes hurt each other's feelings. As the old song said: "You always hurt the one you love, the one you shouldn't hurt at all . . ." Contrary to the more recent idea that love means we never have to say we're sorry, Jesus taught that we *always* have to say we're sorry:

> When you are offering your gift at the altar, if you re-member that your brother or sister has something against you, leave your gift there before the altar and go; first be reconciled to your brother or sister, and then come and offer your gift.
>
> *Matthew 5:23–24*

How many families have relatives not speaking to each other because of some offense or insensitivity of the distant past? How many married couples have placed each other "on hold" because of a long-ago disagreement which was never resolved? How many peo-ple no longer count among their friends someone who at one time was particularly close to them, because of their inability or unwilling-ness to "talk out" an area of hurt and misunderstanding?

Yet, Jesus said to pray, "Forgive us our sins, for we ourselves forgive everyone indebted to us . . ." (Luke 11:4). That is, we sponta-neously ask and expect to be *forgiven,* because we ourselves are *for-giving.* It is important for us to avoid living a "split-level" existence, a two-standard life, in which we always need and ask forgiveness but never forgive. For the marvel of forgiveness/reconciliation to exist, someone must take the initiative. I suppose that in all of our lives there are fleeting pangs of remorse concerning someone we have hurt and also times of pain when we remember someone who has hurt us. If we can learn to honor these times as moments of grace,

moments in which we are being nudged gently to seek or offer forgiveness, there will be fewer people "on the shelf" in our lives, and
many more "neighbors" being befriended.

MATERIAL FOR YOUR REFLECTION

1. *Sacred Scripture*

● I . . . beg you to lead a life worthy of the calling to which you have
been called, with all humility and gentleness, with patience, bearing with one another in love, making every effort to maintain the
unity of the Spirit in the bond of peace. . . . Speaking the truth in
love, we must grow up in every way into him who is the head, into
Christ, from whom the whole body, joined and knit together by
every ligament with which it is equipped, as each part is working
properly, promotes the body's growth in building itself up in love.
Ephesians 4:1–3, 15–16

● Do not forsake your friend or the friend of your parent . . . better
is a neighbor who is nearby than kindred who are far away.
Proverbs 27:10

● . . . a man will leave his father and mother and be joined to his
wife, and the two will become one flesh. This is a great mystery,
and I am applying it to Christ and the church. Each of you, however, should love his wife as himself, and a wife should respect her
husband.
Ephesians 5:31–33

2. *Other Sources*

● Many human beings are obliged to live as celibates. Throughout
the history of humanity, many men and women have not been able

to find the beloved of their hearts. They have lived alone, painfully asking themselves if it is because they are unlovable. For others, the beloved was suddenly torn from them by death. Others entered into the bonds of marriage with the enthusiasm of passionate love, but without the human means for living and deepening the relationship, which eventually broke down. Then, there are all those who carried severe handicaps in their flesh or their spirit. Perhaps they had a fear of relationship, or they had violent or depressive characters. Some had bodies which were mutilated, and others were unable to live a harmonious relationship with another. Many were rejected and devalued. For so many different reasons, they were unable to live a union of love in their flesh. Yet, our experience shows us that when such people live not alone but in community, or in a network of friendship, strengthened and healed by a love which comes from God, it is possible for them to find fulfillment in a life of celibacy.
—Jean Vanier, *Man and Woman He Made Them* (New York: Paulist Press, 1985), 104.

● . . . conjugal love involves a totality, in which all the elements of the person enter—appeal of the body and instinct, power of feeling and affectivity, aspiration of spirit and of will. It aims at a deeply personal unity, the unity that, beyond union in one flesh, leads to forming one heart and soul. . . .
—John Paul II, *The Christian Family in the Modern World (Familiaris Consortio)*, November 22, 1981.

● Personal relationships abound in the priest's life. They are not neatly structured or easily identified and their influence upon him and his spirit is not easily discernible. Such relationships, as understood here, comprise all the significant persons in his life—fellow priests of his own residence or the local presbyterate, both superiors and peers, friends among the faithful, religious and lay, of both sexes, friends not of the household of the faith, both clergy and lay, members of his family, all those people of his past and present whom he has come to know in some depth and who thus are the important people in his life. These persons have become part of him and mediate life to him at every level of his existence. They nourish him by their care and concern; they challenge him by their trust and acceptance.

—United States Catholic Conference, *Spiritual Renewal of the American Priesthood*, 1973, 25.

3. *Moments of Retreat*

Think back to your childhood for a few minutes. Recall childhood friends with whom you shared good times. Ponder the fact that they, perhaps long forgotten, contributed mightily to your developing sense of yourself. Pray in thanksgiving for them and for what they contributed to your young life.

Make a list of the friends you made during your adolescent years and those since. Have you managed to stay in touch with some of them? In your recollection, along with the happy times, are there some regrets? Is there any "unfinished business"? In your journal, sort out some of this, and look for the chance either to reestablish contact in order to reconcile things, or to ask Jesus to help heal the areas of hurt.

Make the choice to pray regularly in gratitude for the friends you have now and those you had along the way of your life. If any of these friends are deceased, or you experience any other grief at the incompleteness of some of your relationships, allow yourself to bring these feelings to Jesus for his gentle healing.

NOTES

1. William Blake, "The Little Black Boy," in *Poems of William Blake*, selected by Amelia H. Munson (New York: Thomas Y. Crowell Company, 1964), 50.

2. Argus Communications (10-27218)
3. Daniel J. Levinson, *The Seasons of a Man's Life* (New York: Alfred A. Knopf, 1978), 99.
4. *Dogmatic Constitution on the Church,* Vatican II, November 21, 1964, #11 (Costello Publishing Company edition, 1975).
5. Thomas J. Tyrrell, *Urgent Longings: Reflections on the Experience of Infatuation, Human Intimacy, and Contemplative Love* (Whitinsville: Affirmation Books, 1980).

BEFRIENDING THE STRANGER

CHAPTER VIII

Befriending the Stranger

"Who is my neighbor?"
LUKE 10:29

Shortly after my ordination in 1963 I visited relatives in my parents' home town, Torrington, Connecticut. After years of little contact with a favorite uncle of mine, a very gentle man with a ready laugh, he and I took a walk. After a while, he began to complain to me about the way the town had changed: "In the old days, you'd pick up the paper, and all the names were Irish and English. Now, they're all *foreigners!*" Claiming the sense of adulthood which ordination can bring, I was brash enough to point out to him that even the Irish and English had come to Connecticut from someplace else!

A couple of years later, Vatican Council II promulgated its *Pastoral Constitution on the Church in the Modern World* and in a section headed "Respect and Love for Enemies" said this:

> Those also have a claim on our respect and charity *who think and act differently from us* in social, political, and religious matters. In fact the more deeply we come *to understand their ways of thinking* through kindness and love, the more easily will we be able to enter into dialogue with them.[1] (Italics added)

To understand the ways of thinking of those who think and act differently from us—how's that for a timely challenge to contemporary followers of Jesus? Notice carefully that this statement of Vati-

113

can II is under the heading, "Respect and Love for *Enemies.*" Interesting—and true! Don't we often count as "enemies" others who merely think or act differently than we do, those who are "foreign" to us? But if we "continue the look of Jesus at the crowd of today," and try to have the eyes and heart of Jesus, as suggested earlier, we will have fewer "foreigners" and enemies in our lives, and many more friends and neighbors.

As we strive to befriend the strangers in our lives, we find that some persons and groups of persons are rather like "personal" strangers, those who tend to engage us "up close" at least in our own emotions, and that others are "global" strangers, those at a greater distance from us. I would like to discuss some of the strangers/enemies in our lives under those two headings, realizing that the distinction between "personal" and "global" strangers is somewhat arbitrary. My approach will be to cite some of the facts and to tell a few of the stories, with the hope that the situations described will urge you to befriend these strangers, at least in your attitudes, at least in your hearts.

I. *Personal Strangers*

HOMELESS PERSONS

One of my boyhood memories is about a one-day family car trip to New York City. As we entered Manhattan from the west side and stopped at a light, a homeless man came up to our car and began wiping the windshield. We were shocked, and later in the day we shared our differing opinions as to whether or not we should have given him some money (we had not done so). A while back, some forty-five years later, while watching *48 Hours* on television, I experienced a contemporary rendition of the same story: a street person washed the windshield of a motorist who took him very seriously, not giving him money, but, seeing in the man's eyes that he really wanted help, giving him his business card. Some months later, the man, now with a home, reported that he had become supervisor of the banquet room of a large New York City hotel, and said, "If the light had been green, I might be dead by now."

My very limited experience of homeless people is that they unsettle me, disturb my heart, remind me of all I have by comparison. It is tempting for me, and perhaps for you, in the midst of our uneasiness, to be judgmental, believing that people are on the streets by reason of their own lack of industry. It is true, of course, that many street people are there because of their dysfunction and the subsequent abandonment of and/or by their loved ones. But it is also true that because of today's economy, many working people are homeless. In Boston, Brian, who works as an account representative for a medical company, is one of hundreds of homeless people in town "who work but cannot afford the substantial sum needed to rent an apartment."[2] Boston has about six thousand homeless persons, and about twenty percent of them are working. When friends want to visit him, Brian tells them that he lives on Cape Cod, since "people don't drop in to Cape Cod for a cup of coffee."[3]

HUNGRY PERSONS

As we walk down the aisles of our modern supermarkets with shelves so fully stocked that the food nearly drops into our carriages, it is hard to remember that many of our own citizens, probably strangers to us, are chronically hungry: "About 20 million Americans, or 1 of every 12, suffers from hunger, according to a 1985 report by Harvard University's Physician Task Force on Hunger in America."[4] The same newspaper article cites a 1977 study by the Government Accounting Office stating that twenty percent of all food is *wasted* as it moves from farm to table. People who work at feeding the urban poor tell us that if the surplus food in every city could be distributed to the poor, no person there would go hungry. Children, especially, are touched by hunger:

> . . . the first nationwide study of the level of childhood hunger in the United States estimates that one child in eight under the age of 12—5.5 million—goes hungry each day

and another 6 million live in families that do not have enough money to spend for food and are at risk of being hungry.[5]

Simultaneously, new products, the lifeblood of the food business, clog the shelves of supermarkets. According to a recent report,[6] more than 12,000 *new* products were introduced in 1989 (1,701 condiments, 1,355 candies and snacks, 1,348 dairy products, 1,155 bakery foods, 913 beverages, etc.). Another report tells us that we Americans can choose from more than 25,000 items in our supermarket, including, in one place, 200 different cereal products—we now suffer from the "overchoice" which Alvin Toffler highlighted in *Future Shock*.[7]

"Overchoice," that is, for many of us—"no choice" for countless others. This cruel situation of some of us being satiated while others go hungry inspires many people across the land to respond creatively to the challenge to feed the hungry. In recent years, for instance, the Boston Walk for Hunger has attracted over 40,000 persons each year who walked twenty miles to satisfy total annual pledges of over $4,000,000.

Countless individuals are doing their part. A friend of mine, Irene Egan, together with her late husband, Tom, and their friends, launched the "Roxbury Food Cupboard," "which collects food and money from churches, temples, schools and private groups to maintain an ongoing inventory for distribution in Roxbury."[8] Early every morning volunteers distribute to the elderly and the poor baked goods which have been donated by food stores and picked up by the other volunteers. The Egans, like many others, were originally inspired by the life and words of Dorothy Day, the great advocate of the poor.

Other persons help in a less formal, "ad hoc" way:

In most ways, the wedding of Barbara [Schwartz] and Abraham [Gutman] on Sunday in Manhattan will be a traditional affair, complete with a white silk gown, a multi-tiered cake and lots of champagne in an elegant hotel. But after the fanfare is over, the couple plan to share their happiness with those less fortunate. They have arranged to have the food that is left over from the reception distributed to the homeless.[9]

Irene Egan, Barbara [Schwartz] and Abraham [Gutman] are among the Americans whose consciences have been touched by the plight of people going hungry in our land of plenty, and who are creatively doing something about it.

DISABLED PERSONS

It is estimated that there are 43 million Americans with a physical or mental disability.[10] Often they have felt second-class, the objects of others' ignorance, prejudice or fear. Only recently has the Americans with Disabilities Act been enacted, bringing hope that this will help things to change.

Government provision for the needs of the disabled is one thing; our personal sensitivity to disabled persons is another. Probably many of us, when we communicate with a disabled person, tend either to make too much of their disability, or to ignore it completely. It is possible for us to be so fixed on the other's handicap that we fail to meet the person. Or it can happen that we are so ill-at-ease because of the disability that we are unable even to acknowledge its presence; again, we miss the person.

Twice I have had the privilege of being a team member for weekend retreats for the disabled. Once my assignment was to drive a young man to and from the retreat. He was paralyzed, and as we sped along the beltway outside Washington, DC, he stretched out on his stomach across the back seat of the car, raising his head so he could see a bit of what was going on. We had lots of laughs that weekend, especially when we returned to the Center where he stayed and no one was available to help carry him in. I did it alone, almost dropping him a couple of times, as he kidded me, "Don't worry, if you drop me I won't break!" In this and other ways, by reason of the way he was, he helped me to know him as a *person*, not primarily as a disabled person.

Another time at the Dominican Retreat House in Schenectady, New York, I had the chance to help a disabled woman with her dessert. To finish her piece of cake she had to more or less clamp onto the fork as I placed it into her mouth each time, and hold on as I withdrew it. Her smile as she finished each mouthful put me at ease. The simple, quiet way in which she allowed me to help reminded me of my reticence in accepting help from those who offer it to me in much less personal circumstances.

Do you recall the last time a disabled person crossed the street in front of you at a traffic light? Whenever I have had that experience I have had a momentary temptation to stare at such persons, but in recent years I have tried rather to notice their quiet dignity, their tangible determination and courage, and I have been strengthened by their gracious example. Whatever I went on to face that day had a fuller dimension to it because of the generosity of heart of the person in the crosswalk.

I wonder if the burdens in the lives of our disabled sisters and brothers are somehow a mysterious part of God's way of bringing strength to us who have disabilities which are more hidden. One thing I know: their gracious presence to the brokenness in their lives connects with our need to own the brokenness in our own lives— deep speaking to deep—and disabled persons who started off seeming like strangers then seemed more like marvelous friends.

PERSONS IN PRISON

Sister Jose Hobday tells a story of an event which took place in the midst of her busy round of talks, travel and correspondence. Once she was between planes at Denver's Stapleton Airport, and after two hours of work on her correspondence, she decided to take a break. Looking around for someone to watch her belongings, she noticed two men nearby:

> They didn't speak at all. The younger man seemed very pleasant and relaxed; he was dressed casually in slacks and a sport shirt. The other, dressed in a suit and looking like a businessman, was quite stern. He didn't smile at all and

paid no attention to anyone, including the man next to him; he struck me as rather dour.[11]

She asked the younger fellow to watch her things, and he readily agreed to do so. After fifteen minutes or so she returned, thanked him, and returned to her writing. Some time later a policeman in uniform approached the two men, and they stood up; only then did she realize that they were handcuffed together, and that the man who had guarded her belongings was the one in custody. As he was being led away, he told her, with a very pleasant grin, that he was being taken in for breaking and entering!

I share this event with you because it resonates with my own recent but limited experience of those in prison: even though, for the most part, they have been guilty of very real offenses, their basic goodness usually shines through. I have met inmates in two different prisons: first, at the Elmira Correctional Facility in upstate New York, where, for three months I celebrated Sunday eucharist with the men there. Rarely has a group paid more attention to my homilies, rarely have worshipers sung hymns with more gusto. And the several men who set up the altar each Sunday and served the mass brought me into closer contact with that group of men to whom Jesus would have been very close.

Second, I have had some connection with the women in MCI (Massachusetts Correctional Institution), Framingham, Massachusetts. Some friends of mine who minister there have formed a faith-community with some of the inmates. To attend one of their informal prayer gatherings is to experience women of very real faith. These women are both a marvelous support to each other and a source of strength to many others in that prison. One Mother's Day evening when I celebrated the eucharist with the wider group of women there, I had a magnificent experience of the church gathered. A talented group of men and women from a Boston parish led the singing, and after mass there was a simple party with soda and a decorated cake, along with a jam session that raised the roof! After the singing and dancing was over, the sister chaplains handed to each woman a yellow rose, donated by a benefactor, and to each mother a

Mother's Day card with a note from a grammar school child—the church at her best: celebration with a group of women to whom Jesus would have been very close.

These are just glimpses of only a few of those who are incarcerated in our country. For all the men and women in prison like the ones I have mentioned, who are able to respond to someone reaching out to them, there are, of course, countless others who can't or won't respond, or who have no one who cares. The statistics are overwhelming, especially those connecting offenses and drugs, and prison life is truly deadening for inmates and personnel alike. Countless prisons have been severely overcrowded for years. Wherever we are, the likelihood is that there are prisoners nearby, strangers in our midst, who need to be befriended, at least in our attitudes.

MINORITY PERSONS

I have not often felt on the "outside," "in the minority." One time, however, on a marvelous trip to Guam for retreats, I had to change planes at the Tokyo airport. I asked for help in finding my plane, and finally was directed to a line marked "aliens." That day, in the minority for one of the few times in my life, I suddenly felt very disconnected from others, very different from them. Some of our citizens have felt on the "outside," like disconnected strangers, for most of their lives. (When I attended Providence College in the 1950s, for instance, there was only one black student there.) Whole groups of people in our society have been distanced by economic factors, by lack of opportunity, and by prejudice—they have been pre-judged on the basis of the color of their skin and/or the place of their homeland.

Crimes of bias have risen in the past few years, and researchers have studied the roots of racism. Dr. Jack McDevitt, a sociologist at Northeastern University who has studied bias crimes in Boston, has said:

> Of all bias crimes, 57 percent involved issues of turf; they were attacks on someone walking, driving through or working in a neighborhood, or on a family moving into the area

or not wanted there. . . . Typical of those was what happened to an Asian family that moved into an all-white neighborhood in Boston. On the first night someone broke several windows with rocks; on the second night the walls were spray-painted with racist slurs. On the third night the family moved back to its old neighborhood, leaving an older son to guard its possessions. A mob of twenty youths taunted the son until he came out, then beat him.[12]

Researchers find that often those who commit these crimes are merely acting out values expressed by family members, and also that attempts to shore up pride in one's own group result in putting down another group—aggression toward a minority group tends to enhance identity with one's own group—and that economic conditions which bring financial crises for poorer people exacerbate things: "Devaluing the other elevates the self: this feeling that I am good is all the more important when you feel your world is out of control."[13] Again, "Economic and political uncertainties lead to personal insecurities. For the most vulnerable people, it's a short step to ethnic violence."[14]

Minority persons, the underclass, the outsiders, the strangers in our midst—for the followers of Jesus, these sisters and brothers of ours present a ready agenda: to bring the values of Jesus concretely into our lives—into our attitudes, conversations and mentalities, and, even more importantly, into our choices, political and personal.

GAY PERSONS

Occasionally I have spoken with men who wanted to talk about the confusion in their lives concerning their sexual identity. Each time I was struck by their sincerity, their genuine search, their ongoing experience of being different. All of them reported their concern when as young men the other guys talked about their attraction to girls, and their own attraction, rather, to their own gender. In other words, rather than having made a conscious, deliberate choice to be homosexual, these men reported that they had merely come gradually to acknowledge an orientation that was at the heart of their very sense of self.

From time to time, too, I have spoken with parents worried about their homosexual son or daughter. The pattern was similar: when faced with the reality, the parents were initially disappointed that their own hopes and dreams for their child would be unfulfilled and terribly concerned for the well-being of their loved one, but gradually they were filled with tender acceptance and a commitment to go on loving.

Things have moved quickly in our society during the past few years, and today there is readier acceptance of gay persons. Acceptance of homosexual relationships is another matter, of course, and the Catholic Church especially has consistently and understandably spoken on the conservative side of the issue. It does seem to me, though, that on a personal level each of us needs a large dose of understanding relative to gay persons. Two sources have added significantly to my own awareness: first, a TV presentation on American Playhouse, "Andre's Mother," a play by Terrence McNally about how a mother (played by Sada Thompson) copes with her son's death from AIDS;[15] second, a poignant story, *The Screaming Room* by Barbara Peabody,[16] another mother's factual account of how it felt to suffer through the difficult death of her gay son.

Whatever the reason, many people who are otherwise exemplary seem to be particularly harsh in their judgments of gay persons. I sometimes wish that they could get to know better some gay person or his or her parents, and listen to their story. I believe that if and when that happened, the gay person would not seem like such a stranger.

II. *Global Strangers*

In addition to the persons above, who tend to engage us up close in some way, there are other strangers—those who are at even a greater distance, geographically and/or culturally, those with lives dramatically different from ours; as we watch our television news, we get surprise glimpses of them, trying to live with dignity in the far-flung corners of the world. Many of them eke out a life of some kind in the midst of a poverty, need and devastation beyond our imagining:

> If the world were a global village of 100 people, one third of them would be rich or of moderate income, two thirds would be poor. Of the 100 residents, 47 would be unable to read, and only one would have a college education. About 35 would be suffering from hunger and malnutrition, at least half would be homeless or living in substandard housing. Of the 100 people, 6 of them would be Americans. These 6 would have over a third of the village's entire income, and the other 94 would subsist on the other two thirds. How could the wealthy 6 live in peace with their neighbors? Surely they would be driven to arm themselves against the other 94 . . . perhaps even to spend, as Americans do, about twice as much per person on military defense as the total income of two thirds of the villagers.[17]

The data is simply staggering. Maybe the plight of the global strangers in our lives will speak most eloquently if I merely share some of the statistics. As you ponder this story of the way things are, I invite you to reflect prayerfully on the harsh reality it presents, and to enter into a thoughtful, gospel-centered reconsideration of your attitudes and choices.

REFUGEES

Fifteen million people, more than ever before, are fleeing their countries, fleeing from both poverty and tyranny. For example, many Vietnamese people have fled to Hong Kong, where "55,000 Vietnamese boat people are confined in camps intentionally kept at minimum survival level to deter further arrivals. 'People are living on shelves,' said the High Commissioner." The same report states: "Civil strife has produced 4.4 million refugees in Africa. The largest single group is 820,000 from Mozambique who have found asylum in Malawi, one of the world's poorest nations.''[18] In fact, Malawi is so poor that as I type its name and the name of many of the poorer countries, my word processor beeps—not as a kind of celebration that these countries exist, but to alert me that I have misspelled their names. In reality, the countries apparently were thought to be either non-existent or so inconsequential that no room was allocated for them in the massive internal memory of my word processor. The word processor beeps if I *misspell* the names of such places as Acapulco, Bermuda, and Cape Cod, but also when I spell *correctly* the names of some of the poorest countries: Benin, Burkina Faso, and Burundi.

CHILDREN

The full page newspaper ad announcing the 1990 World Summit for Children faced us with the eyes of a single child, and the headline: *CHILDREN ARE DYING FOR ATTENTION. 40,000 A DAY.* The piece went on to say:

> Like so many of us, our national leaders are numbed by the enormity of the problem—40,000 children around the world dying each day from malnutrition and disease. Yet, we have within our grasp the means to save almost half of the children under five who die daily—almost 20,000. We have new medical technologies, such as a 10¢ packet of saline nutrients to combat deadly dehydration; we have low-cost vaccines and vitamins, new ways of delivering medicine, and new communication and educational tools to eradicate the ignorance that helps these diseases thrive.[19]

THE STARVING

The eminent sociologist, Sister Marie Augusta Neal, tells the story of starvation in compelling terms. Let me quote at some length from one of her recent books and encourage you to become familiar with her writings:

There is more than enough food in the world to feed the world's people. Despite this fact, a half billion people, one-tenth of the world's population, will die of malnutrition, and 1.1 billion are living in absolute poverty, with their infant mortality rate high and their life expectancy low. Our present response is in the tradition of triage. It includes the following plans, all of which will leave the poor to die: to reduce the production of food that cannot be sold on the world market by paying farmers not to produce it; to continue a policy of planned obsolescence so that those who have access to wealth can discard what they have, purchase more, and keep the economy "healthy"; to continue to exclude struggling third world nations from trade and aid planning groups because of their lack of power and wealth, and thus to continue the production of goods they cannot use and telecommunication systems to which they have little or no access . . . to control the development of independent third world nations on the basis of the harmony or disharmony of their ideologies with the perceived national self-interest of dominating nations; to educate the next generation of children of the non-poor to belief that such action is moral and blessed by God, thereby risking the possibility that these children try to resolve contradictions they experience by escape into drugs, alcohol and suicide in an anomic society.[20]

Does this sound snide and calculating? The story goes on and on—our brothers and sisters across the globe, treated like strangers, treated like enemies, when their only failure has been being born in a poor land:

Eighteen percent of the people live in countries with a developed technology and market economy. These are the twenty-four richest nations, and their per capita GNP stood at $U.S. 7,046 in 1980. Nine other developed countries, characterized by a centrally-planned economy and containing nine percent of the world's people, have an average per capita GNP of $3,091. The remaining, developing countries have seventy percent of the world's population and a per capita GNP of $890 (Population Reference Bureau, 1980).[21]

The sobering news is that the problem is one of *access*, not of capacity to produce food; perhaps this is the ultimate indignity visited upon these global strangers:

> The root of the hunger problem is distribution. In many countries where malnutrition is prevalent, up to half of the cultivated acreage is growing crops for export to those who can afford them rather than foodstuffs for those who need them. Thirty-six out of forty of the poorest and hungriest countries in the world export food to North America (*New York Times,* July 16, 1981, p. A4).[22]

VICTIMS OF WAR AND AGGRESSION

For many Americans, the PBS series on the Civil War, with its black and white still photos, its haunting music and crisp historical commentary brought home to us the horrors of war in a way the more slick media coverage of the Persian Gulf War with Iraq did not. Reports during the latter war were managed, celebrations after the war were orchestrated, and an overwhelming percentage of Americans supported our government's handling of the war. Shortly after the war, the United Nations issued this solemn, terse report: Iraq "for some time to come, has been relegated to a preindustrial age."[23] Also, our Air Force chief of staff "said that during the 43-day Persian Gulf War US planes flew more than 92,000 sorties and dropped 88,500 tons of bombs on Iraq and Kuwait. He said the total included 6,250 tons of precision-guided ordnance."[24] Since the end of the war the truth has gradually unfolded; the outcome, near total devastation. A relatively defenseless people had lost well over 100,000 soldiers, many of them reluctant to fight in the first place. About 25,000 civilians had been killed, and "a Harvard Medical School team estimated . . . [in June 1991] . . . that 170,000 Iraqi kids under five will perish by New Year's, thanks to dysentery, and all the other bugs you get in 110-degree heat when there's no electricity for any but the rich, and all the drinking water comes from a crick where, upstream, people defecated in it."[25] Raw power. Squalor in its wake. Arrogance on a global scale. Hi-tech killing of "enemies" most of whom were, it seems, merely "strangers."

The list of our "strangers," both "personal" and "global," could go on and on. Isn't it true that often we *do* consider them "enemies"? Mostly because they think and act differently than we do? Jesus would want us to embrace them, to "make friends" with them. Perhaps that simple attempt can help set the agenda for our lives in the years to come.

But how about those who *are truly enemies,* either personal or global? How about those who really hate us, abuse us, strike us, are out to do us in? Jesus challenged us with a very demanding ideal—to be non-violent toward them: "Love your enemies . . . if anyone strikes you on the cheek, offer the other also . . ." (Luke 6:27, 29). Hard orders to hear, harder orders to follow; a long way from the "eye for an eye" approach to life, but, through God's grace, often possible in our personal lives, at least.

Loving enemies attempts to keep dialogue open—the conversation continues. Rather than a lifetime of mutual attacks between two people or two families, or long-term or even final distance, never to talk again, loving enemies is disarming—it invites a cessation of harshness. On a societal level, Gandhi and Martin Luther King, Jr. knew about this; perhaps the larger nations still have time to learn it.

Jesus certainly believed in the power of good to overcome evil, the power of the peaceful person to overcome the violent, the power of the disarmed and disarming to overcome those with weapons. Perhaps Jesus was telling us that whenever we offer the other cheek, our enemy might become inclined rather to reach for our hand.

MATERIAL FOR YOUR REFLECTION

1. *Sacred Scripture*

● But wanting to justify himself, (the lawyer) asked Jesus, "And who is my neighbor?" Jesus replied, "A man was going down from Jerusalem to Jericho, and fell into the hands of robbers, who stripped him, beat him, and went away, leaving him half dead. . . . Which of these three, do you think, was a neighbor to the man who fell into the hands of the robbers?" He said, "The one who showed him mercy." Jesus said to him, "Go and do likewise."

Luke 10:29–30, 36–37

● (God) makes the sun rise on the evil and on the good, and sends rain on the righteous and on the unrighteous. . . . And if you greet only your brothers and sisters, what more are you doing than others?

Matthew 5:45, 47

● When the Son of Man comes in his glory, and all the angels with him, then he will sit on the throne of his glory. All the nations will be gathered before him, and he will separate people one from another as a shepherd separates the sheep from the goats, and he will put the sheep at his right hand and the goats at his left. Then the king will say to those at his right hand, "Come, you that are blessed by my Father, inherit the kingdom prepared for you from the foundation of the world; for I was hungry and you gave me food, I was thirsty and you gave me something to drink, I was a stranger and you welcomed me, I was naked and you gave me clothing, I was sick and you took care of me, I was in prison and you visited me."

Matthew 25:31–36

● But I say to you that listen, Love your enemies, do good to those who hate you, bless those who curse you, pray for those who abuse you. . . . If you love those who love you, what credit is that to you?

For even sinners love those who love them. If you do good to those who do good to you, what credit is that to you? For even sinners do the same. If you lend to those from whom you hope to receive, what credit is that to you? Even sinners lend to sinners, to receive as much again. But love your enemies, do good, and lend, expecting nothing in return. Your reward will be great, and you will be children of the Most High; for he is kind to the ungrateful and the wicked. Be merciful, just as your Father is merciful.

Luke 6:27–28, 32–36

● May the Lord make you increase and abound in love for one another and for all, just as we abound in love for you.

1 Thessalonians 3:12

2. *Other Sources*

● In the Christian tradition the commandment to love God and the neighbor is explicitly extended to enemies and strangers (Mt 5:43–48). Theologically speaking, this level of virtue can be attained only with the help of God, by grace. The presence of action, institutions and behaviors that manifest this disinterested love toward strangers and enemies is the stated evidence of conversion won through redemption, itself presented as an act of altruism. The evidence is in the giving of one's life for the other who is not a member of the tribe, who is any stranger with a need. Thus, in the Good Samaritan story, a man who is himself an outcast goes beyond the generosity of the priest and the Levite, taking care of a stranger. . . .
—Marie Augusta Neal, S.N.D. de N., *The Just Demands of the Poor—Essays in Socio-Theology* (New York: Paulist Press, 1987), 58.

● For all our Western individualism and for all our amazement at the lengths to which others take (this) group solidarity, we still retain, consciously or unconsciously, a tremendous amount of group loyalty and group prejudice. It varies from person to person but there are still plenty of people in the Western world who base their identity upon the loyalties and prejudices of race, nationality, language, culture, class, ancestry, family, generation, political party and religious denomination. Love and loyalty are just as exclusive as they ever were. . . .

In the Old Testament to love your neighbor as yourself is to experience group solidarity. Only your kinsman is to be treated as another 'self'. Brotherhood towards some always involves enmity towards others.

Jesus extended one's neighbour to include one's enemies. He could not have found a more effective way of shocking his audience into the realization that he wished to include all people in this solidarity of love. The saying is almost unbearably paradoxical: the natural contradiction between neighbour and enemy, between outsiders and insiders must be overlooked and overcome so that enemies become kinsmen and all outsiders become insiders!
—Albert Nolan, OP, *Jesus Before Christianity* (Maryknoll: Orbis Books, 1978), 60–61.

3. *Moments of Retreat*

Listen again to the words spoken by some of the individuals mentioned in this chapter: "If the light had been green, I might be dead by now." "People don't drop in to Cape Cod for a cup of coffee." "Don't worry, if you drop me I won't break." Now think about the people you met or read about last week, and recall a phrase they may have spoken which resonates in your heart and reminds you of their plight.

As you read newspapers and magazines during the coming week, be aware of the faces of the people you see there. Recognize that many of them are strangers to you, many of them think and act differently than you do. Try not to let them become or remain enemies. Clip a few of the photos of those faces which you find particularly unsettling, and start a "folder of faces."

Many agencies dedicate themselves to the work of reaching out to those who are on the fringe of society and who are particularly needy. Consider writing away for information on the programs of some of these agencies and think about the possibility of joining them in their works:

—Bread for the World: 802 Rhode Island Avenue, NE
                                  Washington, DC 20018
                                  202-269-0200

—Oxfam America: 115 Broadway
                                  Boston, MA 02116
                                  617-482-1211

—Pax Christi USA: 348 East Tenth Street
                                  Erie, PA 16503-1110
                                  814-453-4955

—Covenant House: 346 West 17th Street
                                  New York, NY 10011-5002
                                  212-727-4000

—Amnesty International USA: 322 Eighth Avenue
                                  New York, NY 10001
                                  212-807-8400

—Network: 806 Rhode Island Avenue, NE
                                  Washington, DC 20018
                                  202-526-4070

—8th Day Center for Justice: 1020 South Wabash, Room 680
                                  Chicago, IL 60605-2273
                                  312-427-4351

—Catholic Relief Services:　　　P.O. Box 17090
　　　　　　　　　　　　　　　Baltimore, MD 21298-9664
　　　　　　　　　　　　　　　410-625-6220

—*Maryknoll Magazine:*　　　　Maryknoll, NY 10545
　　　　　　　　　　　　　　　914-941-7590

—*Sojourner Magazine:*　　　　　Box 29272
　　　　　　　　　　　　　　　Washington, DC 20017
　　　　　　　　　　　　　　　202-636-3637

NOTES

1. *Pastoral Constitution on the Church in the Modern World,* Vatican II, December 7, 1965, #28 (Costello Publishing Company edition, 1975).
2. Sally Jacobs, *The Boston Globe,* May 5, 1991, 1
3. Ibid., 4.
4. Michael deCourcy Hinds, *The New York Times,* July 26, 1990, p. A12.
5. Stephen Kurkjian, *The Boston Globe,* March 26, 1991, 3.
6. Eben Shapiro, *The New York Times,* May 29, 1990.
7. Lena Williams, *The New York Times,* February 14, 1990.
8. Jean Dietz, *The Boston Sunday Globe,* January 14, 1990.
9. June Rogoznica, *The New York Times,* May 30, 1990.
10. Steven A. Holmes, *The New York Times,* July 14, 1990. Citing the House-Senate conference report on the Americans with Disabilities Act.
11. Jose Hobday, *Praying* (Beckley Hill, RR 2, Box 4784, Barre, VT 05641), No. 34, p. 31.
12. Daniel Goleman, *The New York Times,* May 29, 1990.
13. Ibid. (quoting Dr. Ervin Staub).
14. Ibid. (quoting Dr. Steven Salmony).
15. DBR Films, 1990.

16. Barbara Peabody, *The Screaming Room* (San Diego: Oak Tree Publications, Inc., 1986).
17. Anonymous; cf. Donnelly/Colt Co., Box 188, East Hampton, CT 06247.
18. Henry Kamm, *The New York Times,* August 12, 1990, 16.
19. *The New York Times,* September 30, 1990. Ad sponsored by *Children's Vigils* (236 Massachusetts Ave., NE #300, Washington, DC 20002)
20. Marie Augusta Neal, S.N.D. de N., *The Just Demands of the Poor —Essays in Socio-Theology* (New York: Paulist Press, 1987), 28.
21. Ibid., 42.
22. Ibid., 44.
23. Trevor Rowe, *The Boston Globe,* March 22, 1991, 14.
24. Ibid.
25. David Nyhan, *The Boston Globe,* August 1, 1991, 15.

CHAPTER IX

Befriending Your Mission

"He sent them out to proclaim the kingdom of God"

LUKE 9:2

In August 1956, as I cleaned out my desk at home before I left for the Dominican novitiate, I came upon a vocation leaflet from Glenmary Home Missioners. I had received it sometime during my grammar school days at St. Joseph's Cathedral School in Hartford, and I had saved it all through my college years. As I looked over the leaflet, I was struck again by its map of the U.S. showing all the counties where there were no priests at all. Looking back now, I realize that that time in grammar school was the first time I had ever thought of being called and of being sent—of mission. I see too that I didn't feel called to serve even in the southern United States, with Glenmary, let alone on the foreign missions. And I'm sure that I saw mission as involving membership in religious orders, and, indeed, in particular communities that had mission as their whole reason for existing.

Vatican II changed my thinking, of course, and this more recent statement by Pope John Paul II finds me enthusiastically on the side of the contemporary emphasis by the church:

Because of each member's unique and irrepeatable character . . . each individual is placed at the service of the growth
of the ecclesial community . . . entrusted with a unique task
which cannot be done by another and which is to be ful-

135

filled for the good of all. . . . Great riches are waiting to be discovered through an intensification of the missionary effort of each of the lay faithful. (This) can contribute greatly to a *more extensive* spreading of the Gospel, indeed it can reach as many places as there are daily lives of individual members of the lay faithful. Furthermore, the spread of the gospel will be *continual,* since a person's life and faith will be one. Likewise the spread of the gospel will be particularly *incisive,* because in sharing fully in the unique conditions of the life, work, difficulties and hopes of their sisters and brothers, the lay faithful will be able to reach the hearts of their neighbors, friends, and colleagues, opening them to a full sense of human existence, that is, to communion with God and with all people.[1]

What a magnificent call to befriend our mission! A vibrant, almost urgent call of the laity to mission—to an incisive, continual, more extensive proclamation of the gospel! The response to such a call will be strengthened, I believe, if we allow ourselves to be touched by those who have missionary hearts. One of them, Tony Breen, a classmate in the order, touched my heart early on with his zeal for mission. He has spent most of his years since ordination in Pakistan; typical of many serving in the far-flung missions, he feels more at home there, it seems, than in his native Rhode Island. Others are on mission stateside: Terry O'Leary, a Sister of the Good Shepherd, who provides home and formation for young mothers and their children in a Boston center; Pat Cheney, a married woman here in my parish in Louisville, who spends herself in sensitive presence to the elderly and the poor; and Liz Gnam, a Dominican, who serves the AIDS prisoners at Trenton State Prison in New Jersey.

They and all the persons I know who have this lively sense of mission have hearts which have been shaped profoundly by the spirit of Jesus. I think of the gospel accounts of mission—of his sending of the seventy-two disciples and the twelve apostles. Let us look closely at the latter account:

He called the twelve and began to send them out two by two, and gave them authority over the unclean spirits. He ordered them to take nothing for their journey except a staff; no bread, no bag, no money in their belts; but to wear sandals and not to put on two tunics. He said to them, "Wherever you enter a house, stay there until you leave the place. If any place will not welcome you and they refuse to hear you, as you leave, shake off the dust that is on your feet as a testimony against them." So they went out and proclaimed that all should repent. They cast out many demons, and anointed with oil many who were sick and cured them.

Mark 6:7–13

So that our hearts may become more fully shaped for mission, let us reflect on some of the nuances of that early missioning:

"Two by two"

Why not alone? It would seem that if they traveled alone, they would be able to get to more places more promptly. Perhaps. But then they couldn't witness to the beauty of relationship and shared ministry—of team. They wouldn't be giving the powerful example of such different persons getting along with one another and complementing each other's diverse gifts.

There are other benefits to being sent in pairs also: *Companionship:* the terrible loneliness that can accompany preaching by oneself would be prevented, and a certain buoyancy might be fostered; as days passed, perhaps they could take turns being "up"? *Clarity and correction:* Jesus realized, of course, that at the time he sent them the new missionaries had only a glimpse of the true message of the gospel, and that they would come to grasp it more fully only along the way. They would need to help each other to sort out and clarify the good news in the very midst of the preaching, as they tried to connect the gospel with the lives of the people they met.

"He ordered them to take nothing for their journey except a staff"

Have you ever wondered why Jesus told them to leave all those things behind? When we draw from each of the gospel accounts, we find that the list of things is rather complete: *Mark 6:* no bread, no bag, no money, only one tunic; *Luke 9:* no staff either; *Luke 10:* not even a purse. The sandals are necessary for the itinerant preacher, who is "on the road," and the staff, allowed in Mark's account, provides for the rigors of the journey.

The things left behind, of course, are things that they would really need. They would need bread to eat; they would need some of the things usually brought in a traveling bag; they would ordinarily need money to provide for unexpected circumstances; they would need a change of tunic or at least a chance to wash their one tunic. But Jesus ordered them to take *nothing* for their journey. What did Jesus have in mind when he sent them out empty-handed like that? I think that Jesus was jealous about the "tone" of their presence, about the way they would be perceived by those who met them, and that he wanted them to be, not self-sufficient, but radically *interdependent*. They who proclaimed the powerful message of salvation would be helped by the people to whom they were sent. It was not a matter of the strong helping the weak, the smart helping the dumb, the able helping the unable—they were all learners, they all had the same teacher, and they were to help each other and minister to each other in an environment charged by mutuality.

"Wherever you enter a house, stay there until you leave the place" (and: "remain in the same house, eating and drinking whatever they provide. . . . Do not move about from house to house"—Luke 10:7)

It seems as though Jesus was saying, "be satisfied with what is given to you, *whatever* is provided, whether it be sumptuous or spare. Don't be seeking out those who can provide more lavish meals and lodging, because then you will be a counter-witness, presenting yourselves in a manner inconsistent with the gospel of grace which you are preaching. Don't be manipulative of the people to whom you are sent; rather, be truly *receptive*, open, and able to accept from those who welcome you and offer you what you need." Jesus was concerned that on their mission they be perceived as being sent for *all,* not just for the well-off.

"If any place will not welcome you and they refuse to hear you, as you leave, shake off the dust that is on your feet as a testimony against them"

What is at stake here? I believe that Jesus is concerned about the quality of their presence in the *next town* to which they journey. He does not want them to seem like people who have been "done in" or diminished by their mission to the previous town. They should take care of themselves, always ready to make a fresh start in the new place, not weighed down by whatever disappointments or failures they may have experienced in the last place.

This factor, of being in shape for the mission, demands a communal sense of humor, a light touch, a willingness to allow God's grace time to work in the hearts of those who hear the message of salvation. It demands the awareness on the part of those on mission that they have *been sent* by another, that the message they proclaim is the message of the one sending them. And they dare not take themselves too seriously, thinking or acting as though they are the ones really responsible for the message being heard. Only when this light touch is present will their manner be consistent with the good news proclaimed, the healing given.

Some preachers I know took Jesus at his word. They had preached at all the masses in a particular parish church one weekend, inviting the people to scripture sharing sessions and prayer in the homes of the parish during the week ahead. The preachers had prepared carefully for and participated generously in the daily gatherings, yet they experienced very limited success. The people of that parish did not respond. So as the preaching team left that parish at the end of the week, they stopped their car at the town line, got out, and shook that town's dust from their clothes! And they arrived in the next town without the burden of failure which otherwise might have been theirs; they arrived relaxed, happy, and ready to preach the good news afresh.

Befriending Your Mission Today

After the resurrection of Jesus, on the same day that he had appeared to the two disciples on their way to Emmaus, he appeared to the eleven and their companions in Jerusalem:

> While they were talking about this, Jesus himself stood among them and said to them, "Peace be with you." They were startled and terrified, and they thought that they were seeing a ghost. He said to them, "Why are you frightened, and why do doubts arise in your hearts? Look at my hands and my feet; see that it is I myself. Touch me and see; for a ghost does not have flesh and bones as you see that I have." . . . In their joy they were disbelieving and still wondering. . . . Then he opened their minds to understand the scriptures, and he said to them, "Thus it is written, that the Messiah is to suffer and to rise from the dead on the third day, and that repentance and forgiveness of sins is to be proclaimed in his name to all nations, beginning from Jerusalem. You are witnesses of these things. And see, I am sending upon you what my Father promised; so stay here in the city until you have been clothed with power from on high."
>
> *Luke 24:36–39, 41, 45–49*

The Holy Spirit, the promised power from on high, was sent on the day of Pentecost, and Pentecost is an eternal mystery—the Holy Spirit continues to come into our lives. How important for us, then, not to remain frightened and filled with doubts, *disbelieving and still wondering;* how important for us to agree to be proclaimers, witnesses; to agree to our sending, our mission. An attitude of remaining self-enclosed, huddled in fear as the early disciples were before the coming of the Spirit, is inappropriate, for the Spirit has come! Rather, we need to claim the power from on high, and to get on with the very important tasks of our mission.

Contemporary Christians are coming in greater and greater

numbers to an awareness of the powerful truth that mission is for everyone—we are all sent to be proclaimers of the reign of God. This is properly seen as a call to adulthood and to a role which is fully adult in the mission of Jesus and in the ministry of the church. Needs continue to cry out for attention, creative possibilities continue to present themselves, and ministries are expanding as the church attempts to meet the demands and opportunities of this moment. At the same time, numbers of clergy and religious continue to dwindle. Even if this were not so, lay ministry should, of course, be developing strenuously, but since it is so, there is a special urgency to this moment; this is truly a moment of grace for the church.

Let me mention only four of the many areas in which the need for adult Christians on mission is especially critical:

1. *Marriage and Family Life*

It is of crucial importance for parents and spouses to witness to the possibility of living healthy, coherent lives as mothers, fathers, wives and husbands, and to minister directly to the many other spouses and parents who seem not equal to the task. The world around us seems not to believe in the possibility of having a healthy married and family life, seems to despair of its happening. Family life is in crisis; even the affluent are poor when it comes to the benefits of a healthy home life. One out of every two marriages is breaking up. Even those marriages which last are often only a shadow of what they are meant to be, with spouses sharing facilities and a certain history, but not really sharing their selves, the deeper aspects of who they are as unique persons. For followers of Jesus to settle for that kind of marriage relationship is for them to settle for far too little.

2. *The Local Parish*

In a very real sense, if renewal is not taking place in our own parish, it might just as well not be taking place anywhere. It does not really help to know that other parishes are being renewed if in our own parish contacts are impersonal, liturgy is lifeless, programs are uncreative, and the style of leadership is listless. Vatican II had a different dream, a dream of fully adult parishioners participating actively in the life and plans of their parish. The council even noted that parishioners "refresh the spirit of pastors."[2] Some pastors welcome having their spirits refreshed, and they seek out the ideas, creative suggestions and expertise of their people. Others do not. When the pastor is secure with himself as a man and as a priest, where the pastor himself is fully adult, the people flourish, because in an ongoing, creative fashion, he is able to invite others to share their gifts.

Where the pastor is insecure as a man and/or as a priest, the scene is one of control, distance, manipulation, harshness, and criticism of those who have different ideas from the person "in charge" of "his parish." Often pastors who are insecure do not even make a nod in the direction of collaborative ministry. Look closely at a parish where people are crowding the place, and where there is a real team approach to life, with laity, religious, deacons and other priests warmly accepted as full-fledged members of the parish staff, and you are looking at a parish with a pastor who is secure.

Over the past several years, people have been "voting with their feet," leaving their neighborhood parish in search of one where they could be really nourished. Others, in order to be fed, have flocked to retreat houses and renewal centers. Often the ones who search elsewhere are the more creative, dedicated people. If there is hope for the parish, it rests, of course, in its parishioners staying and contributing to a style of ministry and worship which is truly enriching—parishioners in a sense looking upon their own parish as "mission territory," a place to which they are being "sent" in a new way.

When I was a vocation director, I spoke one time to the campus minister at the University of Connecticut. He told me how hard it was for the students to make the transition to their home parishes during the summer. Late each spring he held a special "debriefing" session in which he warned them of the challenge ahead and coached them on how to speak to their priests at home about what might be lacking and about what they needed. He encouraged them, when possible, to offer their own services in ways that would be helpful. At the time I was saddened that all of this was necessary, but I was also happy to realize that these young people already had a wonderful sense of mission to their own parishes.

3. *Foreign or Domestic Missions*

One of the glories of the present moment is the number of lay people who are engaged in the missionary life of the church on either a permanent or a transitional basis. Some of them are associate members of one of the religious communities with foreign missions (e.g. Maryknoll) or one with stateside missions (e.g. Glenmary Home Missioners). In each of their lives there is both a marvelous new personal outreach and a magnificent contribution to the works and spirit of the particular institute.

4. *Volunteer Activity*

Sometimes I meet people whose lives are relatively simple, who have become quite self-enclosed. I often suggest to them that they consider some kind of volunteer commitment. Befriending one's mission can be as simple a thing as being attuned to the possibilities for service in the midst of the exact circumstances of one's life at a given moment. "What are the needs, who are doing without what they need, and where does the gospel send me this day?" We're surrounded by opportunities to serve, whether it be a one-time offer to elderly neighbors to mow their lawn or an ongoing pledge to collect day-old supermarket bread for distribution to the hungry.

If we're tuned in to people in our parish, and let it be known to parish leadership that we are available to help, that's a marvelous contribution to parochial life; it can quicken the awareness of the whole parish, and before long we have a parish whose communal psyche is shaped by an alertness to those in need. Consider the suburban Boston parish mentioned earlier which has thirty people who regularly visit prisoners in addition to those providing music for the prison liturgies.

Newspapers in many large cities publish a weekly list of volunteer opportunities. Simply reading your daily paper with an eye to lending a hand where needed is a wonderful way to live. Consider it a moment of grace when, as you read a story, you are struck with concern and feel nudged to help; make a prompt phone call and soon you may be engaged in an ongoing mission of mercy. For instance, a while back I came upon a piece which told of two architects who had donated their services to redesign a brownstone in Manhattan for The Variety House for Children, one of the residential treatment centers for young children born with AIDS or cocaine addiction. The report states that the place is "cozy and full of whimsical details, like wood cabinets inlaid with animal motifs and floor tiles that form a whale."[3] The executive director of the Association to Benefit Children, which sponsored Variety House, said:

> There are 300,000 children a year who are born to crack addicts. These children are born with blindness, deafness, kidney and brain damage. We have to over-structure them, over-warm them, over-kiss them.[4]

One of my friends said it well: "Being a volunteer is the rent I pay for living on this planet."

We, the disciples of Jesus in the contemporary world, spend our lives, then, befriending our mission, agreeing to be sent the way the early disciples were sent. We go forth with others, sharing our gifts, proclaiming the gospel by our words and the witness of our lives. We "take nothing" for our journey: we agree to go empty-handed, relative to the awesome needs we encounter. When we feel inept, we honor that sense of powerlessness, and rejoice in the awareness that often our witness is simply to have a "solidarity in powerlessness" (Henri Nouwen) with those to whom we are sent. All along the way we accept the welcome and the help and the ideas of those to whom we are sent. We develop a "light touch" which helps us to "keep on keeping on," (the favorite saying of Regis Ryan, a priest friend with multiple sclerosis); we refuse to hold back because of fear, with the awareness that then we would be taking ourselves a bit too seriously, and the promises of Jesus not seriously enough. And every day, whatever the nature of our mission, we witness to the love and healing care of Jesus, and live our lives in a manner consistent with the example of all those who have gone before us, "clothed with power from on high" (Luke 24:49).

MATERIAL FOR YOUR REFLECTION

1. *Sacred Scripture*

● As in one body we have many members, and not all the members have the same function, so we, who are many, are one body in Christ, and individually we are members one of another. We have gifts that differ according to the grace given to us: prophecy, in proportion to faith; ministry, in ministering; the teacher, in teaching; the exhorter, in exhortation; the giver, in generosity; the leader, in diligence; the compassionate, in cheerfulness.

Romans 12:4–8

● You are the light of the world. A city built on a hill cannot be hid. No one after lighting a lamp puts it under the bushel basket, but on the lampstand, and it gives light to all in the house. In the same way, let your light shine before others, so that they may see your good works, and give glory to your Father in heaven.

Matthew 5:14–16

● But you are a chosen race, a royal priesthood, a holy nation, God's own people, in order that you may proclaim the mighty acts of him who called you out of darkness into his marvelous light. Once you were not a people, but now you are God's people; once you had not received mercy, but now you have received mercy.

1 Peter 2:9–10

● The gifts he gave were that some would be apostles, some prophets, some evangelists, some pastors and teachers, to equip the saints for the work of ministry, for building up the body of Christ, until all of us come to the unity of the faith and of the knowledge of the Son of God, to maturity, to the measure of the full stature of Christ.

Ephesians 4:11–13

● Let us not grow weary in doing what is right, for we will reap at harvest-time, if we do not give up. So then, whenever we have an opportunity, let us work for the good of all, and especially for those of the family of faith.

Galatians 6:9–10

● The love of Christ urges us on . . .

2 Corinthians 5:14

2. *Other Sources*

● Sister Dorothy Kazel, O.S.U., a native of Cleveland, was slain with three other American missionaries on December 2, 1980. The following reflection was written by Cheryl Kazel, one of her nieces:

I am Sister Dorothy Kazel,
Missionary to El Salvador,
Harbinger of God's Good News.

With heart and hands open to the needy
I came to serve those in servitude.
I came to preach the Gospel of Peace
To those staggering under the yoke of injustice.
Day by day I comforted the sorrowful
Fed the hungry, sought out the helpless,
Rescued the refugees and consoled the children.

I planted the seed of hope
In hopeless hearts
And watered it with tears of compassion.
But I was not destined to see that seed flourish,

For the fruit does not always fall
To the planter of the tree.

Hatred, prejudice, and brute force
Combined to snuff out my life
Far from home, family and friends.

Now I am an eternal Alleluia,
Forever praising the Tri-une God,
Forever holding the poor of El Salvador
In my heart.

—Dorothy Chapon Kazel, *Alleluia Woman* (Cleveland: Chapel
    Publications, P.O. Box 210107, Cleveland, Ohio
    44121, 1987), 53.

- *From a friend on mission in the Dominican Republic:* "There are so
  many with critical medical problems who need to see doctors in
  the capital. We subsidize almost everyone who goes. Donation
  money also goes for medicine, prenatal vitamins, emergency food,
  lots of things. We've even paid for coffins and are low on sheets
  ourselves as we've given them for burials. One of the most heart-
  wrenching stories for me was a man to whom we'd given money to
  bring his two-year-old to the hospital in Las Matas. The man returned the next week to repay a part of the trip (not expected) and
  told us the child had died, and since he couldn't afford what a
  carpenter asked for a coffin, he made one himself using the front
  door of his home . . ."
  —Sister Carolyn Sullivan, OP; Hondo Valle, Dominican Repub-
    lic; December 1990.

- If we learn anything from the witness of Christ we learn that life is
  a parable: our own plans are always being overthrown. This is the
  case not only in our personal lives but in our corporate efforts at
  ministry as well. Our best "authorizations" fall eventually under
  scrutiny and require purification. Metaphors that had once

seemed so divinely inspired—our life together imaged as a hierarchy, our leaders pictured exclusively as male celibate clergy—reveal their shadow side. The authorizing of certain structures of ministry represents our best efforts to respond to the patterns of God's power that Jesus has recognized for us. But these efforts always await purifying. The reforms of the Second Vatican Council and the subsequent decades provide an excellent example of an effort to purify past authorizations of ministry and leadership. Our courage to continue this purifying process enables us to contribute to the ongoing cycle of empowerment that is Christian life in the world.

—James D. Whitehead and Evelyn Eaton Whitehead, *The Emerging Laity—Returning Leadership to the Community of Faith* (Garden City: Doubleday & Company, Inc., 1986), 149.

● In Melbourne I paid a visit to an old man no one knew existed. I saw that his room was in horrible condition and I wanted to clean it up, but he stopped me: "I'm all right." I kept quiet, and finally he let me go ahead. In his room was a beautiful lamp, covered with dust. I asked: "Why don't you light the lamp?" He replied: "What for? Nobody comes to see me, and I don't need a lamp." Then I said to him: "Will you light the lamp if the Sisters come to see you?" "Yes," he said, "if I hear a human voice, I will light it." The other day he sent me word: "Tell my friend that the lamp she lit in my life burns constantly."

—Mother Teresa of Calcutta, *The Love of Christ—Spiritual Counsels* (San Francisco: Harper & Row, 1982), 31.

3. *Moments of Retreat*

Do you have a "lively consciousness" of your responsibility for the world? Is there in your life some regular outreach to the needy of your area? Is there some way you might cooperate in the foreign mission activity of the church? Pray over these matters as you assess the level of your response to mission.

Do you know someone who has a "missionary heart"? Is that person involved in some program of helping others with which you might connect yourself?

When you experience disappointments and limits in your life of witness to the gospel, are you able to "shake the dust off"? Spend some time reflecting on this question and journaling. Ask yourself whether or not you sometimes drag along with you the incompletenesses of yesterday.

What is your level of involvement in your parish? Is there some way in which you might be part of things in a way which is more fully adult?

NOTES

1. John Paul II, Post-Synodal Apostolic Exhortation *On the Vocation and the Mission of the Lay Faithful in the Church and in the World* (*Christifideles Laici*), December 30, 1988, #28.
2. *Decree on the Apostolate of the Laity,* Vatican II, November 18, 1965; #10 (Walter M. Abbott, SJ edition).
3. Elaine Louie, "For Babies With Little Else To Smile At," *The New York Times,* July 5, 1990.
4. Ibid.

CHAPTER X

Befriending the Earth

"God saw everything that he had made,
and indeed, it was very good"

GENESIS 1:31

After the Iraqis left Kuwait, setting afire over seven hundred oil wells, media crews filmed the ensuing devastation. Ever since, there have been periodic reports about the terrible impact this has had on the environment. The moment has been emblazoned on our memories forever. It might serve to remind us that for many years we have been ravishing the earth and pillaging its resources. The exploitation of the goods of the earth and the consequent negative impact on our environment is one of the central issues of our time.

Father Thomas Berry, who has devoted much of his life to fostering reverence for creation, says it very well:

As we think our way through the difficulties of this late twentieth century, we find ourselves pondering the role of the human within the life systems of the earth. Sometimes we appear as the peril of the planet, if not its tragic fate. Through human presence the forests of the earth are destroyed. Fertile soils become toxic and then wash away in the rain or blow away in the wind. Mountains of human-derived waste grow ever higher. Wetlands are filled in. Each year approximately ten thousand species disappear forever. Even the ozone layer above the earth is depleted. Such disturbance in the natural world coexists with all those ethnic, political and religious tensions that pervade the human realm. Endemic poverty is pervasive in the Third World, while in the industrial world people drown in their own consumption patterns. Population increase threatens all efforts at improvement.[1]

We humans have come, then, to imperil the planet on which we live. Is it not important for us, rather, to learn again how to befriend the earth? For our earth is the place where we respond to God's befriending love, and learn to love our God, ourselves, and our neighbors. In that response to our creator's love we learn to appreciate and care for the wondrous work of God's hands. It is essential that the tone of our lives, the attitude with which we relate to God, ourselves, and our neighbor, be consistent with the attitude with which we relate to the earth, God's handiwork, as are we. We reflect now, then, on our call to befriend the earth.

I would like to consider, first, God's original design; next, the nature of our response; then, how to recover a sense of wonder and respect for creation; finally, some practical steps that we can make in this matter.

I. *God's Design: Genesis Revisited*

The sacred text tells us: "In the beginning when God created the heavens and the earth, the earth was a formless void and darkness covered the face of the deep" (Genesis 1:1–2). As the days of creation unfolded, God created, successively, light, sky, earth, seas, plants yielding seed, fruit trees, the two great lights (sun and moon), swarms of living creatures (great sea monsters and winged birds), cattle, creeping things, and wild animals. Then God created humankind:

Then God said, "Let us make humankind in our image, according to our likeness; and let them have dominion over the fish of the sea, and over the birds of the air, and over the cattle, and over all the wild animals of the earth, and over every creeping thing that creeps upon the earth."

Genesis 1:26

After blessing humankind, God said to them:

"Be fruitful and multiply, and fill the earth and subdue it; and have dominion over the fish of the sea and over the birds of the air and over every living thing that moves upon the earth."

Genesis 1:28

A commentator on Genesis has stated that to write out the original thirty-five verses of Genesis, "Israel's faith required centuries of carefully collected reflection," and that these verses convey "ancient, sacred knowledge, preserved and handed on by many generations of priests, repeatedly pondered, taught, reformed and expanded most carefully and compactly by new reflections and experiences of faith."[2]

The marvel of creation, such a wide panoply of creatures coming from God's hand, each having the power to propagate itself, and pronounced, at the end, "very good" by their creator! The issue at hand is, of course, the specific response of the human creature to God's words: "have *dominion* . . . over every living thing that moves upon the earth" and "*subdue*" the earth.

A scripture scholar points out that to subdue suggests "to bring forcefully under control. Force is necessary at the beginning to make the untamed land serve humans. Humans nonetheless are to respect the environment; *they are not to kill for food* but are to treat all life with respect."[3] (Italics added)

But later in the sacred text we find a change:

God blessed Noah and his sons, and said to them, "Be fruitful and multiply, and fill the earth. The fear and dread of you shall rest on every animal of the earth, and on every bird of the air, on everything that creeps on the ground,

and on all the fish of the sea; into your hand they are deliv-
ered. *Every moving thing that lives shall be food for you;* and
just as I gave you the green plants, I give you everything.
Only, you shall not eat flesh with its life, that is, its blood.
(Italics added)

Genesis 9:1–4

So things change:

There is a qualification of the original blessing: the conces-
sion that the originally vegetarian humans may kill animals
for food, including fish and fowl. . . . The qualification of
the original blessing is not because of divine miscalculation
in the initial creative act . . . but because of God's willingness to bear with sinfully violent humans.[4]

Or, as stated in similar fashion, "the prohibition [against
bloodshed] is modified in the renewal of creation after the flood
(Genesis 9:2–5) because of the disobedience and violence mysteriously present in the human heart."[5]

The original blessing qualified, God's willingness to bear with
sinfully violent humans, modification because of the disobedience
and violence mysteriously present in the human heart . . . and things
have never again been the same.

II. *Our Response: "The Sighing of the Creature Begins"* [6]

God's original design suggested an all-encompassing peace and
the ongoing gentle presence of humans to the rest of creation. God's
plan was for stewardship, not strangulation. God's hope was for befriending, not violence and fierce manipulation. But humans sinned;
sibling is slain by sibling; disobedience, alienation and toughness
enter in. So in chapter 9 of Genesis, God's original design is altered:
now, "What God's address takes simply for granted is a severe

disruption and degeneration of creation, which came forth from God's hand as 'very good.' "[7]

In our own day, when the astronauts looked back on earth and took photos of our strikingly beautiful planet, things have come to crisis. Books are written about the peril which has come to our earth; periodicals warn us of the crisis which looms. The data is deadening in its impact. Consider just a few of the countless statistics:

—Since the dawn of the industrial age, some six million chemical compounds have been synthesized by man. Of these, at least 70,000 are now in common use, with over 1,000 new chemicals entering the market every year. The vast majority are xenobiotic, that is, 'alien to life.' "[8]

—The Earth possesses a staggering diversity of plant and animal life. To date, biologists have classified almost 2 million species, but recent research suggests that the final count could top 40 million, insects alone accounting for 30 million species. But as we have set out to conquer nature, subjugating one ecosystem after another to our perceived needs, so species after species is being wiped off the face of the planet.[9]

—The vast expanses of the North American Great Plains were once home to 60 million bison . . . in the 1860's, the Europeans arrived and a wholesale slaughter began. Killing bison for their hides and tongues, they reduced the seemingly unlimited herds to just 500 animals within 40 years. The Indians and their rich cultures were similarly devastated by the white men's quest for land and profit. By 1876, they had been pushed onto reservations, a defeated and broken people.[10]

—The average city dweller in the US consumes about 125 gallons of water, 3.3 lbs. of food, and 15.6 lbs. of fossil fuels per day, and generates about 100 gallons of sewage, 3.3 lbs of refuse, and 1.3 lbs of air pollutants. New Yorkers produce enough garbage every year to cover Central Park to a depth of 13 feet.[11]

As each year passes, the areas of concern multiply: the ozone layer continues to be depleted, with consequent global warming; tropical countries are deforested at an alarming rate; meat continues to be over-consumed by first world people, meaning that animals are fed, but humans are deprived of the grain which could have kept them alive; chemicals are used in such a way as to diminish the health of agricultural land; rivers and seas are polluted; coral reefs are destroyed; marine life is trapped indiscriminately. All of this makes life itself precarious for many of the world's people and diminishes the quality of life for countless others. "The sighing of nature" continues in earnest, a nature which deserves to be befriended.

III. *Recovering a Sense of Wonder*

It is the call of the creature to attend to the world of the creator with a sense of awe and wonder. How terrible for a human to stand only in dulled awareness of a universe filled with miracles. How marvelous for a person to echo a song of praise to the giver of all such good gifts, bringing gentle presence, creative stewardship, and a deeply-rooted spirit of befriending to an earth beset with perils, but still magnificent.

Ours is an age of exploding awareness into the intricacies and vastness of the universe. Every day in some vehicle of the popular press there is new information about the world which can nudge the thoughtful reader into a stance of wonder. Consider several recent reports:

> On the clearest of nights, high in the cool, dry mountain air, the unaided human eye can glimpse perhaps 6,000 objects in the sky: individual stars, a few planets and a multitude of galaxies composed of millions of stars but so far away that they appear as single points of light. Through the most powerful optical telescope, the "Big Eye" on Mount Palomar in California, with its 200-inch mirror, astronomers can make out as many as 40 billion objects and also

recognize the magnificent architecture of galaxies chained together as super-galaxies spanning the sky.[12]

The article quoted above goes on to say that with the launching of the Hubble Space Telescope, the vision of astronomy was expected to be expanded tenfold, "bringing into focus 5 to 10 trillion objects." As the Hubble was deployed, an editorial appeared titled "Harvesting the Universe," saying that as data was gathered, "astronomers will recalculate the age and structure of the universe, and so refine their theories of its origin and evolution."[13]

As we know, the Hubble experiment was flawed, but the data continues to gather:

—Astronomers have identified what they think is the largest galaxy ever observed, more than 60 times the size of the Milky Way. . . . The galaxy, embracing more than 100 trillion stars . . . is a distinct galaxy more than six million light years in diameter. . . . The Milky Way, Earth's home galaxy, is about 100,000 light years wide.[14]

—The solar system may contain about 1,000 planets, not just the nine that are now known, according to a new theory. . . . Untold numbers of Pluto-sized planets may have orbited among the known planets after the solar system's birth almost 5 billion years ago and now may circle so far away from the sun that they have yet to be detected. . . .[15]

This kind of data boggles the mind. And it accumulates at an amazing pace, not regarding only the heavens, but even concerning the age of the universe. Father James W. Skehan, a Jesuit scientist who lectured at our spiritual life center in Dover, Massachusetts, startled some of us a while back by reminding us that the eastern coast of Massachusetts closely matches the rock formations on part of the western coast of Africa, and that the continents were at one time contiguous land masses, and also by telling us that the lovely rock ledges on the Priory grounds were over 600 million years old!

The explosion of data continues, in *every* possible area of science and of human research. For instance, consider:

> Ants "are the little creatures who run the world . . . they represent the culmination of insect evolution, in the same sense that human beings represent the summit of verte-brate evolution." Ants have been evolving 100 million years longer than humans, and it shows. Because all the ants in a colony are closely related—they have the same queen as a mother—they tend to act in the interest of the whole. Ants are altruistic; with chemical signals secreted from glands, they share information (where to find food or the enemy, which ants to feed). Some ants store food in giant, expand-ing stomachs to be regurgitated to others in times of need. Self-sacrificing ants explode in the face of an enemy, cover-ing it with poison from a long gland that also summons recruits to battle, usually the oldest soldiers (younger ants are left behind to care for families).[16]

The heavens, the earth, the variety of species of all living things, the intricate design at the heart of all that is created—all of this continues to beckon to the thoughtful believer, calling us to reflec-tion, awe, wonder, and praise. If we are appreciative enough about what is, the hope is that we will find our days, our lives, echoing a continual hymn of praise, a stance very appropriate for followers of Jesus, the one who always pointed out the wonders of the world around them to those who followed him.

IV. *Practicalities of Befriending the Earth*

What to do? How to respond to this moment? Thomas Berry, the priest and geologian mentioned above, is among those who offer creative, radical solutions to the crisis of an earth being done in: "What is our personal task at this moment? What to do individually is determined by the competencies of a person. We must follow our own competencies."[17] He points out the need to stop the present destruction, and applauds activist groups such as Earth First. Berry argues for the refusal "to repair the infrastructures of the industrial establishment," and predicts that future generations will necessarily have to live among the ruins we have come to create.[18] Although I rarely think about our present crisis in such cosmic terms, my awareness is heightened by those who do.

For most of us, much of the time, our focus will probably need to be on a more "daily," more mundane level—developing a more simple lifestyle, saving energy at home and on the road, raising the consciousness of our family and friends, recycling all that can be used again—striving to be open to God's design for us and for the earth now. So that these and other possibilities do not remain simply good ideas, you might choose to provide yourself with one of the simple aids currently available. Let me suggest the following ones, which have come to my attention over the past few months:

—*50 Simple Things You Can Do To Save the Earth* [Earth Works Press, 1400 Shattuck Ave., #25, Berkeley, CA 94709, 1991]. (Provides background data in fifty areas of concern, and a list of practical activities to help save the earth.)

—*Household Hazardous Waste Wheel* [Environmental Hazards Management Institute, 10 Newmarket Road, P.O. Box 932, Durham, NH 03824]. (A listing of waste categories for household and auto products, paints and pesticides, along with their hazardous ingredients; this also provides a very helpful list of "alternatives.")

—*The Complete Guide to Recycling at Home—How To Take Responsibility, Save Money, and Protect the Environment* [Gary D. Branson, Betterway Publications, Inc., P.O. Box 219, Crozet, VA 22932, 1991]. (Among the appendices are lists of books, magazines and resources which focus on the matters at hand, organizations which promote environmental causes, and manufacturers who provide catalogues of their environment-friendly products.)

These and many similar aids to environmental befriending are available in most bookstores and in many public libraries. Perhaps by perusing them and by communicating their message to family and friends, you will help quicken others' dedication to appreciating God's design, to responding to the "sighing of the creature," to recovering a sense of wonder at the marvels of creation, and to meeting in healthy and creative fashion the crucial need to befriend our earth.

MATERIAL FOR YOUR REFLECTION

1. *Sacred Scripture*

●   Bless the Lord, my soul.
    O Lord my God, you are very great. . . .
    You stretch out the heavens like a tent,
    you set the beams of your chambers on the waters,
    you make the clouds your chariot,
    you ride on the wings of the wind,
    you make the winds your messengers. . . .
    You set the earth on its foundations, so that it will never be
      shaken.
    You cover it with the deep as with a garment. . . .
    You make springs gush forth in the valleys;
    they flow between the hills, giving drink to every wild animal;
    the wild asses quench their thirst.
    By the streams the birds of the air have their habitation;
    they sing among the branches.
    From your lofty abode you water the mountains;
    the earth is satisfied with the fruit of your work.
    You cause the grass to grow for the cattle,
    and plants for people to use. . . .

The trees of the Lord are watered abundantly. . . .
In them the birds build their nests. . . .
O Lord, how manifold are your works!
In wisdom you have made them all;
the earth is full of your creatures. . . .
Bless the Lord, O my soul. Praise the Lord!

Psalm 104, passim

●   Yours is the day, yours also the night;
you established the luminaries and the sun.
You have fixed all the bounds of the earth;
you made summer and winter. . . .
Have regard for your covenant,
for the dark places of the land are full of the haunts of violence.
Do not let the downtrodden be put to shame;
let the poor and needy praise your name.

Psalm 74:16–17, 20–21

●   The heavens are yours, the earth also is yours;
the world and all that is in it—you have founded them.
The north and the south—you created them;
Tabor and Hermon joyously praise your name.

Psalm 89:11–12

● You have forgotten the Lord, your Maker, who stretched out the
heavens and laid the foundations of the earth.

Isaiah 51:13

● . . . the creation waits with eager longing for the revealing of the
children of God; for the creation was subjected to futility, not of
its own will but by the will of the one who subjected it, in hope that
the creation itself will be set free from its bondage to decay and
will obtain the freedom of the glory of the children of God. We

know that the whole creation has been groaning in labor pains until now; and not only the creation, but we ourselves, who have the first fruits of the Spirit, groan inwardly while we wait for adoption, the redemption of our bodies.

Romans 8:19–23

● Look at the birds of the air; they neither sow nor reap nor gather into barns, and yet your heavenly Father feeds them. . . . Consider the lilies of the field, how they grow; they neither toil nor spin, yet I tell you, even Solomon in all his glory was not clothed like one of these.

Matthew 6:26, 28–29

2. *Other Sources*

● The gifts of creation have been given to us to nurture, to protect, to preserve; these gifts also preserve, protect and nurture us. In our day-to-day lives, there is much we can do to act as responsible stewards of God's handiwork.

Through saving energy. Adequately insulate your home. Keep furnaces operating at top efficiency. . . . Keep your automobile, preferably a smaller, gas-efficient and emission-safe model, in top running condition. For short trips, walk!

Through recycling. Buy beverages in returnable containers; bring empty bottles and cans to your supermarket or claim center. Work with municipal and state authorities to implement community-wide recycling programs.

Through parenting. Raise "global Christians" by educating your children about the needs of others around the world and how we are all dependent on each other.

Through your lifestyle. Live as simply as possible. Plant a vegetable garden. Use what you have as long as you can. Re-sole a pair of shoes instead of buying new. Avoid disposable items: paper towels, plastic utensils (they're made of petroleum!). Buy cards made from recycled paper. Re-use the bags you get at the grocery

store. Do without unnecessary appliances such as electric can-
openers and knives.

Through cooperation. Join community-based groups that work
to conserve resources, to save and protect the environment.

Through prayer. Daily prayer opens us to God's guidance
about how we can serve as God's instruments on the earth God
created. . . .

—"What on Earth Can I Do?" from *Christopher News Notes* (New
York: The Christophers, February 1990), #322.

● We cannot discover ourselves without first discovering the universe, the earth, and the imperatives of our own being. Each of
these has a creative power and a vision far beyond any rational
thought or cultural creation of which we are capable. Nor should
we think of these as isolated from our own individual being or
from the human community. We have no existence except within
the earth and within the universe.

—Thomas Berry, *The Dream of the Earth* (San Francisco: Sierra
Club Books, 1988), 195.

● Nothing is more tragic or pitiful than the statements of Indians
who have survived to see their sacred lands torn up and dese-
crated by a people of an alien culture who, driven largely by com-
mercial interests, have lost the sense of protective guardianship
over nature. Typical are the words of an old Omaha:

"When I was a youth, the country was very beautiful. Along
the rivers were belts of timberland, where grew cottonwood, ma-
ple, elm, ash, hickory, and walnut trees, and many other shrubs.
And under these grew many good herbs and beautiful flowering
plants. In both the woodland and the prairies I could see the trails
of many kinds of animals and could hear the cheerful songs of
many kinds of birds. When I walked abroad I could see many
forms of life, beautiful living creatures which *Wakanda* had placed
here; and these were, after their manner, walking, flying, leaping,
running, playing all about. But now the face of all the land is
changed and sad. The living creatures are gone. I see the land

desolate and I suffer an unspeakable sadness. Sometimes I wake in the night and I feel as though I should suffocate from the pressure of this awful feeling of loneliness."

—Melvin R. Gilmore, *Prairie Smoke* (New York: Columbia University Press, 1929), 36. Quoted by Joseph Epes Brown in *The Spiritual Legacy of the American Indian* (New York: Crossroad, 1988), 40.

3. *Moments of Retreat*

Read prayerfully the first chapter of the book of Genesis. Jot down phrases that prompt an attitude of befriending the earth. Spend some time pondering whatever implications suggest themselves for your life.

Reflect upon the distinction between *subjugation* and *stewardship* of the earth. Are there ways in which you might become more of a steward of the earth and its resources? For instance, ways in which you might make additional creative plans for recycling?

Check your local library for books which tell about the wonder of the universe: perhaps an atlas, a travel book or a science text. Look for any copy of the *National Geographic;* pray over its pages, its photos, especially its people and their surroundings.

Consider buying a calendar which will highlight for you during the year the awesomeness of creation. As a suggestion, look for the yearly calendar prepared by the artist Mary Southard, CSJ. Follow the thoughtful approaches to daily prayerful practices that she suggests. To obtain the latter calendar, write to:

Calendar
Sisters of St. Joseph
1515 W. Ogden Avenue
La Grange Park, IL 60525-1798
708-354-9200

NOTES

1. Thomas Berry, *The Dream of the Earth* (San Francisco: Sierra Club Books, 1988), 6.
2. Gerhard Von Rad, *Genesis—A Commentary*, rev. ed. (Philadelphia: The Westminster Press, 1972), 63.
3. Richard J. Clifford, SJ, "Genesis," in *The New Jerome Biblical Commentary* (Englewood Cliffs: Prentice-Hall, 1990), 11.
4. Ibid., 16.
5. Ibid., 11.
6. Von Rad, 131, quoting Otto Procksch, *Die Genesis,* 3rd ed. (Leipzig: A. Deichert, 1924).
7. Von Rad, 130.
8. Edward Goldsmith et al., *Imperiled Planet—Restoring Our Endangered Ecosystems* (Cambridge: The MIT Press, 1990), 32.
9. Ibid., 36.
10. Ibid., 118.
11. Ibid., 241.
12. John Noble Wilford, *The New York Times,* April 9, 1990, 1.
13. Editorial, "Harvesting the Universe," *The New York Times,* April 26, 1990.
14. John Noble Wilford, *The New York Times,* October 26, 1990.
15. David L. Chandler, *The Boston Globe,* May 30, 1991, 4.
16. E.O. Wilson and Bert Hölldobler, quoted by Elizabeth Royte, *The New York Times Magazine,* July 22, 1990, 19.
17. Thomas Berry, CP, in dialogue with Thomas Clarke, SJ, *Befriending the Earth—A Theology of Reconciliation Between Humans and the Earth* (Mystic: Twenty-Third Publications, 1991), 112.
18. Ibid., 112–113.